THE KIDS BEHIND THE LABEL

THE KIDS BEHIND THE LABEL

An Inside Look at ADHD
for Classroom Teachers

TRUDY KNOWLES

HEINEMANN
PORTSMOUTH, NH

Heinemann

A division of Reed Elsevier Inc.
361 Hanover Street
Portsmouth, NH 03801–3912
www.heinemann.com

Offices and agents throughout the world

The author and publisher wish to thank those who have generously given permission to reprint borrowed material:

Figure 1.1 reprinted with permission from *Diagnostic and Statistical Manual of Mental Disorders*, Fourth Edition, Text Revision. Copyright 2000, American Psychiatric

Library of Congress Cataloging-in-Publication Data
Knowles, Trudy.
    The kids behind the label : an inside look at ADHD for classroom teachers / Trudy Knowles.
        p. cm.
    Includes bibliographical references.
    ISBN 0-325-00967-8 (alk. paper)
    1. Attention-deficit-disordered children—Education—United States.
    2. Hyperactive children—Education—United States.   I. Title.
        LC4713.4.K57 2006
        371.94—dc22   2006006024

Editor: Lois Bridges
Production editor: Sonja S. Chapman
Typesetter: Gina Poirier Design
Cover design: Night & Day Design
Manufacturing: Steve Bernier

Printed in the United States of America on acid-free paper
10   09   08   07   06   EB   1   2   3   4   5

To Rob
It is a joy being your mom.

In memory of Don Keller
Don was one of the wisest people I've ever known.
He was always willling to share his deep wisdom with me.
Don truly understood and loved Rob. I miss him.

LETTERS
By Rob

ADD/ADHD
This plethora of letters
They all describe me
Can't pay attention
It's messing with my education
But do you really care?

Every morning I wake up and down four pills
Just so I can stand in line and finish all your drills
Maybe if you opened up your eyes you'd see
You don't have to do what's already been done to me.

ADD/ADHD
This plethora of letters
They all describe me
Can't pay attention
It's messing with my education
But do you really care?

No One's Ever Asked Me Anything
Before the school psychologist started the evaluation with me, she asked me a couple questions about myself, how I feel going through school, what my experiences had been. With the few things I told her she said, "A lot of these are typical of symptoms or signs of someone with ADD. This is really surprising that no one' s really noticed this before." And I said, "Well, no one's ever asked me anything."

—KRISTINA

An Apology
I feel sorry for a lot of my teachers who taught me over the years. I caused them much frustration.

—GRANT

Contents

Foreword

*I'm asking you to treat all children as though they were yours;
to love them, treasure them, and guide them with tenderness;
to build relationships, listen, and be helpful. . . . Nothing is more
important—not test scores, not grades, not a quiet,
controlled classroom . . . than having that child leave your
classroom feeling lifted up and loved.*

—TRUDY KNOWLES, *THE KIDS BEHIND THE LABEL*, p. 128

The world of special education has long been dominated by clinical perspectives that equate learning and behavior "problems" with specific deficiencies that reside "in people's heads." In this formulation, Attention-Deficit/Hyperactivity Disorder (ADHD) is seen in terms of an array of neurological and/or behavioral deficits that limit students' capacity to focus their attention and/or control their impulses which, in turn, interfere with their ability to function in school. Remedial efforts usually focus on "fixing" students with some combination of medication and explicit, behavioral interventions (e.g., strategies for increasing self-control), although discussions of ADHD often include suggestions for various classroom modifications and adaptations.

Curiously, the discourse of special education, while invoking the language of individualization, is informed by research literature that focuses its attention on a statistically-constructed "average" student. Case studies that present the profiles of individual students have been published, but such accounts are rare. Rarer still are opportunities for educators, parents, and researchers to hear the actual voices of students with special needs. In this context, *An Inside Look at ADHD* is a wonderful gift. Trudy Knowles' interviews with fourteen young men and women who exhibited symptoms of ADHD from an early age give a human face to ADHD. Knowles is herself the mother of a son with ADHD whose story is "one of struggles, phone calls, conferences, incomplete work, tears, depression, homework undone, projects unfinished, books unread, detentions, arrests, suspensions, drugs" (p. 2). But this isn't her story. From the young men and women she interviewed we learn how students *experience* Attention-Deficit/

Hyperactivity Disorders. We learn what it means to be distractible, disorganized, and impulsive from the perspective of people who live with these symptoms. More importantly, we learn what these people desired from their teachers. Certainly they appreciated curricular adaptations and modifications, but above all they cherished teachers who cared about them personally, teachers who wanted them to succeed and challenged them with meaningful, thoughtful curriculum, teachers who were simply "nice." Here's how Trudy Knowles sums it up.

> Time and time again the storytellers said that what they wanted was to be seen as a human being with thoughts, feelings, ideas. They wanted to be treasured for the gifts they brought to the classroom, not demeaned for not being able to do it the way everyone else does. They wanted to be listened to—not just the words that were said but also the words that weren't said. (p. 58)

Too often these young men and women with ADHD experienced classrooms firmly entrenched "in a world of strict accountability, report cards, standardized tests, and state mandates. . . . classrooms where organizational skills and conformity to one way of learning and thinking dominate" (p. 129). Teachers ruled by inflexible standards and one-size-fits-all curricula were unable to meet the personal and educational needs of these students. But students with ADHD are not unique in that respect. Schools don't fit lots of students. Schools don't fit students who enter school not quite ready to read. Schools don't fit many poor and minority students as evidenced by the so-called achievement gap. Schools don't fit students whose first language is not English. Schools don't fit girls who often find math and science classes inconsiderate of their preferred ways of learning. Lately, a lot of attention has been given to boys who frequently find schools hostile to their interests and more active learning styles (Smith and Wilhelm, 2002; Newkirk, 2002).

To the degree that rigid structures of schooling fail to accommodate the needs of vast numbers of students, meeting the needs of students with ADHD is part of a much broader challenge: creating classrooms that are congenial to the range of ways students learn and live their lives. All students have a right to flexible, challenging, and interesting curricula that respond to their individual needs. All students covet respect and understanding. All students want teachers who are "nice." Creating classroom structures considerate of the needs of students with ADHD demands schools and classrooms that take account of the social, cultural, and learning needs of ALL students. Instead of getting children ready for school, we need to imagine getting schools ready to serve the increasingly diverse population of students in our classrooms (Swadener, 1995). We owe a debt of gratitude to the men and women who generously shared their thoughts with Trudy Knowles for giving us a better sense of what truly inclusive classrooms might look like.

—Curt Dudley-Marling
Boston College

References

Newkirk, T. (2002). *Misreading Masculinity: Boys, Literacy, and Popular Culture*. Portsmouth, NH: Heinemann.

Smith, M. and J. Wilhelm (2002). *Reading Don't Fix No Chevys: Literacy in the Lives of Young Men*. Portsmouth, NH: Heinemann.

Swadener, B. B. (1995). Children and families "at promise": Deconstructing the discourse of risk. In B. B. Swadener and S. Lubeck (eds.), *Children and families 'at promise': Deconstructing the discourse of risk* (pp. 17–49). Albany, NY: State University of New York Press.

Acknowledgments

Sometimes I feel like the treasure in a chest that hasn't been opened yet.

—Don Keller

This book has been a labor of love for years. When my son, Rob, was going through school, I was the parent from hell, pushing for his right to have an education full of meaning and joy despite his diagnosis of ADHD. My heart would fill with pain when he came home from school feeling defeated and that he was just not good enough. I made a promise to myself that I would never give up on helping people understand that all children are precious and have a right to be lifted up. That is what this book is about.

The greatest joy in writing this book was the chance to sit with so many people and listen to their stories. The storytellers were willing to open up their hearts and lives to me. I thank Jessie, Grant, Jillian, Jennie, Jill, Belkies, Nicholas, Dave, Kari and her mom, Kristina and her mom, Brandon and his mom, and Geoff and Nick and their mom. What a thrill it was to enter their lives. And thanks to Theresa who shared stories of her son over dinner.

One of the storytellers has a special place in my heart. I have known Jessie all of her life. She has made me laugh and made me think. And she's grown up to be a beautiful young woman.

I have had four wonderful graduate assistants who have helped me throughout the years. Thanks to April Nadolna, Stacy Adams, Erin Boutin, and Terry Portenstein. They interviewed, researched, edited, proofread, and most important, transcribed tapes—a thankless task. Terry was there at the end, typing, researching, formatting, and giving me last-minute support. She was amazing and I thank her.

I have been blessed to have worked with and been supported by great colleagues. Their passion for education and their dedication to great teaching is always an inspiration. A special thanks to my colleague Peggy Sullivan, an amazing teacher who never stops advocating for students and thinks that all of her students are wonderful.

Thanks to Nancy Doda for being my friend. She believes in me and because of that belief I am able to do what I do. I cherish her. Thanks to the rest of the Madison Crew: Jim Beane, Barb Brodhagen, Carol Smith, Ann Yehle, Dave Braun y Harycki, and Bill McBeth. They are all amazing educators who believe strongly in giving students a voice. It is an honor to work with them.

Special thanks to my editor Lois Bridges. She believed in this project from the beginning and she's the one that finally made it happen.

Nothing is more important to me than my family. They have always supported me in all of my projects and have supported and loved Rob his whole life. My mom and dad loved me unconditionally and helped me believe in myself. I thank them and miss them terribly.

Thanks to my sister, Anne Snell. She was willing to tell her story and give me editing advice. Her support has been so important to me. Her constant encouragement gave me the courage to finish this book. She is an incredible educator. It's always fun to talk education with her.

Thanks to my brother, Mark Knowles. He's also written books and I don't care. He's talented, funny, and makes me laugh.

Thanks to my brother, Rex Knowles. He didn't help me with this book but we did fight over a birthday cake once and I think it ended up on the floor. He helps me in so many ways with his wisdom and strength.

Thanks to my sister, Nancy Lund. She is the most generous person I know. Her gentle spirit guides me.

My in-laws also deserve thanks—Sherry, Larry, Keith, and Don. They are such a huge part of my life and Rob's life. My nieces and nephews—Juliet, Jessica, Eric, John, Canedy, Jessie, Suzie, Steve, and Daniel—have also been a big part of Rob's life. They are so full of love, more than tongue can tell.

My children deserve the most thanks. First I want to thank Rob. He's the reason I'm writing this book. Rob's my youngest child. He has enriched my life and brought me great joy. One day I was sitting with Rob at the doctor's office. We were watching a two year-old, with an attention span of about five seconds, bounce off every wall in the waiting room. Rob turned to me and said, "I hope when I have kids they have ADHD. It's so much fun." And it has been—not necessarily easy but a whole lot of fun. Rob struggled throughout school and continues to try to figure out this thing we call life. It's been a great journey.

My four other children—Mellissa, Rachel, Austin, and Ariel—are all amazing people. This book is for their brother. They've put up with him all these years and have loved him fiercely.

And thanks to Dan, my anchor and my friend. He accepts me exactly as I am, chaos and all. He makes me laugh when laughing is the hardest.

Speaking From
the Heart

As a toddler, he lost every babysitter he ever had. He was faster, smarter, and could stay awake longer than any of them.

Once he entered school, the calls started coming. By first grade the teacher was calling about once a week trying to figure out what to do with him. He was constantly disrupting the class and talking out of turn. One day she said, "I finally figured it out. I put him at a table with three little girls who never say anything. It's working." Despite his behavior, that year he received an award for being the best all around academic student in the classroom.

His second-grade teacher said, "I have neither the energy nor the desire to figure out what to do with him in class." The third-grade teacher couldn't figure out whether he belonged in a class for gifted students or for students with behavior problems. In the fourth grade, he was always losing points on his papers because he would forget to put his name, or the date, or the subject on them and the papers were usually late. Each of those was minus ten points. He sat down at the kitchen table in tears one day and asked, "When did I get to be so dumb?" Later that year he came home and said, "I wanted to jump in front of a truck instead of having to go to school one more day." He didn't go back to the fourth grade.

He struggled academically through the fifth grade and finally in the sixth grade, he was diagnosed with Attention-Deficit/Hyperactivity Disorder–Combined Type. Thus began his six-year struggle with finding a medication that would help and an education that was meaningful.

In the seventh grade, he worked one night for four hours on a science project. Because of handwriting and spelling disabilities, the project wasn't perfect. He received a grade of 73 with the comment, "Be more careful. Take your time." His response: "I worked four hours on this project. If I had worked for ten minutes I would have gotten a seventy-three." He never worked hard in school again.

In the eighth grade, he suffered severe depression and had to be put on a homebound tutoring program. In the ninth grade, he came home from school two weeks before Christmas and said, "I'm not going back. You can't make me go back to school. You could tie me to a chair and I would leave school with that chair still tied to me." He again finished the school year in a homebound tutoring program.

In the tenth grade, he left his school district and went to a performing arts high school where he encountered teachers who saw the gifts he brought with him. He loved those teachers and that school but by then he was broken. He struggled through the next three years. Although he found success with drama and music, the academic work never became meaningful. He found himself constantly in trouble for any number of reasons: being late for class, leaving campus to go to the store, leaving in the middle of class, convincing kids to leave class with him, smoking in the bushes behind the school, not doing his work. Six weeks before the end of his senior year, he appeared before an expulsion board that decided, although they didn't want him back on campus, he could finish his work at home so that he could graduate. The director of the school couldn't pinpoint one big event that led to the expulsion hearing, describing it as, "Death by 10,000 thumbtacks."

He finished his work at home and when they called his name to receive his diploma, he cried. One by one, he fell into the arms of the president of the Board of Directors, the two teachers who had been chosen to represent the senior class, and the two cofounders of the school. "It's over," he said later. "I'll never have to do this again."

As his mother, I never realized the depths of the agony that going to school produced for him. I should have known. I knew him when as an infant he never slept, when as a toddler he could clear a table or a bookshelf faster than I could clean it up. I should have known when I watched him struggle every year for thirteen years of school. I was at the school or on the phone, sometimes daily, talking to teachers or principals. I saw the homework. I saw the report cards. I knew his frustration. I just didn't know the agony. I am a teacher-educator and the mother of a twenty-two-year-old son with Attention-Deficit/ Hyperactivity Disorder (ADHD). Rob's story is not uncommon. He's intelligent, creative, talented, funny, and an all around nice guy. Yet his story is one of struggles, phone calls, conferences, incomplete work, tears, depression, homework undone, projects unfinished, books unread, detentions, arrests, suspensions, drugs. He's my own son and yet I didn't know what to do.

"What can teachers do to help you?" I would ask him. And always the answer was the same, "They could listen to me. I just want someone to listen to me."

I wanted to create a handbook for teachers to give them help in developing strategies for ADHD students. After I conducted numerous interviews, I realized I couldn't write a book filled with strategies. Who was I to tell other teachers what strategies would work? And anyway, teachers know what these strategies are. They know about color-coding folders and giving written instructions, about untimed tests and breaking work into smaller pieces, about leniency with late papers and doing oral work instead of written, about being patient and having a sense of humor. Yet, teachers still feel frustrated and students still feel failure.

What started out as the desire to write a book filled with strategies for teachers has developed into a joyous journey of discovery. You see, I thought I knew what was best for students with ADHD. After all, I was a professional educator and the mother of a son with ADHD. Then I began to interview. I had the opportunity to talk with and to listen to a number of students and young adults who have been diagnosed with Attention-Deficit/Hyperactivity Disorder. I wanted to find out what school was, or is, like for them and what could have helped make it better. As I interviewed, I found myself doing what my son had always wanted: I began to listen, to hear, and to understand.

My plans for this book changed form. I decided to let the storytellers speak for themselves. In the book, you will still read the history of ADHD and be presented with strategies that work; however, more important, you will be hearing the voices of young people with ADHD.

The Storytellers

This book is written from the frame of reference of fourteen individuals who were chosen for interviews because they exhibited symptoms of ADHD from an early age. They have all struggled to make meaning out of their education and continue to search for meaning in their lives. Twelve of them have an official diagnosis of Attention-Deficit/Hyperactivity Disorder. One is in the process of being evaluated. One is self-diagnosed.

It is their stories that can help everyone understand the nature of ADHD and how it impacts not only school success but also life in general. These storytellers, along with four of their mothers, shared their lives with me so that teachers can begin to understand who they are and what is in their hearts and minds.

Let me introduce them to you.

Kari, an Eight-Year-Old Third Grader

Kari was in the third grade when I interviewed her and her mother Sheila. Kari's symptoms were first noticed at the end of first grade during which she was constantly moving, blurting out answers, and talking out of turn. She was diagnosed with ADHD in the second grade. She was having difficulty focusing on her work and attending to the teacher. Kari's mom told me that Kari "wants people to realize that she is not doing things to misbehave or to be bad or because she doesn't understand the rules. She can't control it."

Marti and Her Sons Nick and Geoff

Marti is the mother of three sons with ADHD. Alex, her oldest, is an artist. He was not interviewed for this book.

Nick, Marti's Twenty-Year-Old Son

Nick began having trouble in school during the fourth and fifth grades. He had difficulty getting work done and was distracted by the noise in the classroom. Things really began going downhill in middle school. He spent two years in the eighth grade during which his achievement was inconsistent and he began daydreaming in class. Part way through his freshman year in high school, he was diagnosed with ADHD and put on a 504 Plan with a tutor with whom he worked every day. He played JV soccer and baseball that he said "kind of kept me in line and made me focus on getting things done."

Nick had to go to summer school after his junior year because he flunked math. His senior year didn't go well at all. As he described it, "By the senior year everything kind of meshed together in my head, all the bad things that had happened." One day, about two-thirds of the way through his senior year, he left high school and never went back. He said he just couldn't bring himself to go anymore. Nick's dream is to play baseball. He wants to get his GED and maybe enroll in college.

Geoff, Marti's Twenty-Four-Year-Old Son

Geoff had been working as a cabinetmaker for three years when I interviewed him. He began his struggles with school during the first grade when he became, as his mother said, "increasingly resistant to going to school." He was diagnosed with a reading disability and stayed in a Title I program through middle school. His diagnosis of ADHD came during a summer school class in high school. Geoff remembered telling another student that he never could retain what he had just read. The other student said that the same thing used to happen to him and he had been diagnosed with ADHD. Geoff was soon diagnosed by his doctor and has been on medication ever since. His story about the red pencil can be read in Chapter 5.

Belkies, a Twenty-Nine-Year-Old College Senior

Belkies was born in Puerto Rico and moved to the United States during high school. She remembered always being in trouble in kindergarten. Throughout elementary school her mom was at the school frequently. Belkies' grades were bad, and she was always talking and forgetting things. She failed some classes in the seventh grade, mostly because she couldn't sit down to do the work. She described herself as being distracted by movement and sound, with her thoughts all over the place. She got involved in sports because, "I was so hyper all the time that it gave me an escape."

Belkies spent five years at a community college but left one credit short of an Associates Degree. She transferred to a four-year college where she has been for five or six more years. She continues to struggle in college, often starting the semester well but then really having to push herself to go to class at the end.

Kristina, a Seventeen-Year-Old High School Junior

Kristina, whose mother Melanie sat in on the interview, was a sophomore in high school when she received her diagnosis of ADHD. She said elementary school wasn't that bad but she started going downhill in middle school. Her mother, however, said the problems started around the third grade when she was told that her daughter was reading below grade level. Kristina just did not seem to be listening to or following instructions. By the tenth grade, she was failing every class. More of Kristina's story can be read in Chapter 4.

Brandon, a Fourteen-Year-Old Ninth Grader

Brandon was interviewed with his mother Suzan. She said she first noticed hyperactive behaviors when he was a toddler. "He just didn't sit still and he would constantly be into everything all over the place." Brandon was diagnosed with ADHD when he was in kindergarten. He started taking medication and was able to sit for the first time and do work. Brandon has struggled throughout school; he called himself a "troublesome student bully, getting up in class and trying to glue the teacher to the seat, cutting a girl's hair, punching other kids."

At the time of the interview, Brandon was not on any educational plan. He wasn't eligible for an IEP and his mother said, "The school refused to give me a 504 Plan." She is constantly frustrated with what she thinks is the school's inattention to Brandon's problems. She feels like it is starting to come together, but she is the one that has had to do the pushing. Since middle school, Suzan said, "It's just one big fight after another. This is stuff that shouldn't be happening. It's been like this throughout Brandon's entire school life."

Brandon goes to a vocational-technical high school where he likes electronics class because "we do mostly labs and I'm doing good in it." Brandon felt like teachers didn't give him help in school. He said, "The teachers do not care at all. At least in this high school they don't. Only one of them makes me try and think."

Grant, a Twenty-One-Year-Old College Student

Grant, who is currently studying film and directing, was diagnosed with ADHD during the seventh grade but said that he had never done well in school. He said, "I think my first signs of it were in elementary school around third or fourth grade. I would always have trouble completing tests and assignments, especially math." About middle school he said, "It got to the point . . . where I was just sick of school already and I hated going. I never was really hyper. I've always been kind of relaxed but just not able to concentrate."

During high school, Grant went for three years to a Quaker school that he described as a "tiny school out in the middle of the woods." The personal attention he received from teachers there helped him to be successful. During his senior year, he was involved in a program where he traveled around the country with nine other students and one teacher. He said he learned more that year than any other year. Grant tells the story of that trip in Chapter 7.

Jessie, a Twenty-One Year-Old College Senior

Although Jessie was not diagnosed until her sophomore year while studying theater in college, she has struggled with symptoms for her whole life. During elementary school, she frequently got in trouble for talking and daydreaming in class. Things got worse for her in high school. Her story can be read in Chapter 11.

Nicholas, a Twenty-Two-Year-Old College Senior

Nicholas, who is studying engineering, was diagnosed with ADHD in the third grade when teachers were concerned about him not completing work they felt he was capable of doing. Despite the diagnosis, Nicholas said that he did verily well in school but that he never did reach his potential.

After high school he went to a community college for a semester and then took a semester off. The following year he went away to a small college for a year then transferred to a university for the engineering program. Nicholas says that even now he doesn't ever study and hates to read. His biggest problem continues to be his inability, as he says, "to buckle down."

Jillian, an Eighteen-Year-Old College Freshman

Jillian was diagnosed with ADHD midway through her sophomore year in high school primarily due to impulsivity and hyperactivity. She recalls that elementary school wasn't that bad but she feels that she "must have spaced out during most of it because I don't know some of it now (like fractions)." She described herself as "always doing something," and she calls herself a very good multitasker, except when she's on medication and can only do one thing at a time. Jillian said, "I always knew there was something different about me. I couldn't learn a certain way that most kids could." Jillian is studying to be a teacher.

Jill, a Nineteen-Year-Old College Sophomore

Jill has not had an official diagnosis. When she went for counseling in college, the counselor showed her a list of the symptoms of ADHD and Jill said she had all of them except for one. Her family doctor will be giving her a referral for further evaluation.

Jill has always had difficulty organizing her thoughts and staying focused in class. She said in elementary school she didn't have a clue what was going on "all the time." She remembers being in what she thinks was a resource room. In high school she said, "I'd always get in trouble for talking. I could never raise my hand and wait on the teacher. I'd always have to yell it out and I'd always interrupt." If she was interested in something, she could do the work very well, but if she was not interested, her attention would wander. Jill is also studying to be a teacher. More of her story can be read in Chapter 4.

Dave, an Entertainer

Dave is self-diagnosed. He said, "I haven't had those official tests, however, having read a bunch of the books on ADD, I realize that I struggle with a load of those issues. There is a checklist with a hundred questions and I got 95."

Dave remembers his early education as being frustrating although he was really bright. He described himself as somewhat of an outsider. He developed many strategies for making it through school, such as locking himself in his bedroom to do homework or going into the woods to write a paper.

After high school, Dave started college but finally gave up and dropped out. He moved to Europe and later New York City where he has been a performer for more than twenty years.

Jennie, a Twenty-One-Year-Old College Senior

Jennie was diagnosed with ADHD in high school. She said she just felt that something was wrong with her because she spaced out all the time, couldn't concentrate in class, and had trouble sitting still. During elementary school she struggled with reading and concentrating, lost things, and as she said was, "always bouncing up and down." She is studying to be a teacher. Her story can be read in Chapter 3.

Rob, Interviewed Twice

He is my son and was interviewed as a fourteen-year-old middle schooler and an eighteen-year-old high school senior. Rob was officially diagnosed with ADHD when he was in the sixth grade. His symptoms began, however, when he was a toddler. He was creating chaos faster than it could be cleaned up. School was a struggle for him for the entire time. He had difficulty sitting still, focusing, or completing work.

Interview Transcriptions

A short comment about the interview transcriptions: Interviewing people diagnosed with Attention-Deficit/Hyperactivity Disorder was both a joyous and an interesting experience. Some of their sentences went on for two single-spaced pages. The rambling thoughts are symptomatic, take a long time to transcribe, and are difficult to interpret. For some of the quotes in this book, I have taken the liberty of cutting out portions of the ramblings that didn't pertain to the idea or theme.

I've cut out a lot of "like, you know" or incomplete thoughts that were spoken before the complete thought was formulated. For some of the quotes, I rearranged the sentences to add to the understanding and flow of the thoughts. I have stayed true to everyone's ideas.

Listen to the storytellers' words because the story is theirs. The children with ADHD are not the problem. In their beauty, wonder, activity, and creativity, they are the solution. And in reading their stories, you will begin not only to understand them, but also to love them. Despite the very real frustrations of teaching ADHD students, you can create classrooms where every child is welcomed and every child is given a chance to succeed.

Attention-Deficit/Hyperactivity Disorder is a label. It can be a valuable label if it helps teachers understand what's going on in the lives and minds of their students who are challenged with ADHD. It can be a valuable label if it helps children understand themselves better. The label can help them realize that they are not lazy or bad and that there is nothing wrong with them. A number of the storytellers felt relief that they finally had a label to help explain what they had felt all their lives.

ADHD is the label. I invite you now to meet the kids behind the label.

What Is 2 ADHD?
Like a Ping-Pong Ball Shooting Everywhere

A Brief History

Attention-Deficit/Hyperactivity Disorder (ADHD) is a neurological disorder characterized by impulsivity, hyperactivity, and inattention. Although the exact number of people in this country with ADHD is unknown, estimates range from 2.5 to 10 percent of the population—10 to 25 million people. That means there are one or two diagnosed and/or undiagnosed ADHD children in every classroom.

It is not a new phenomenon as some contend. Humans who have exhibited excess activity, inattention, and impulsivity have probably been around forever. Who knows what became of them? I think, knowing what I know now, they might have been the great hunters or warriors of their time. They might have been the first to play with fire, the first to confront a wild boar, or the first to step into or out of the forest to discover a new way of living. Maybe they boarded a boat when the world was flat and headed to the horizon, or crossed the great American prairie to see what was on the other side. I believe that they invented, experimented, and created; that they became mystics and shamans, seeing visions and dreaming dreams; and that because of their excess activity, inattention, and impulsivity, we have all benefited.

German physician Heinrich Hoffmann, who wrote a number of verses for children during the 1840s, first described ADHD in the literature more than a century and a half ago. His story of Fidgety Philip seems to be the first written account of attentional problems and hyperactivity.

The Story of Fidgety Philip
by Heinrich Hoffmann

"Let me see if Philip can
Be a little gentleman;
Let me see if he is able
To sit still for once at table."
Thus spoke, in earnest tone,
Thus Papa bade Phil behave
And the mother looked very grave
But Fidgety Phil
He won't sit still
He wriggled
And giggled,
And then, I declare,
Swings backward and forward
And tilts up his chair,
Just like any rocking horse;
"Philip! I am getting cross!"
See the naughty restless child
Growing still more rude and wild.
Till his chair falls over quite.
Philip screams with all his might,
Catches at the cloth, but then
That makes matters worse again.
Down upon the ground they fall.
Glasses, plates, knives, forks and all.
How Mamma did fret and frown.
When she saw them tumbling down!
And Papa made such a face!
Philip is in sad disgrace.
Where is Philip, where is he?
Fairly cover'd up you see!
Cloth and all are lying on him;
He has pull'd down all upon him.
What a terrible to-do!
Dishes, glasses, snapt in two!
Here a knife, and there a fork!
Philip, this is cruel work.
Table all so bare, and ah!

Poor Papa, and poor Mamma
Look quite cross, and wonder how
They shall make their dinner now.

Hoffmann also wrote "The Story of Johnny Head-in-Air," which describes a child with attentional problems without hyperactivity. He's describing the child we've all seen who looks out the window, stares into space, and then says, "What was it you said?"

The Story of Johnny Head–in–Air
by Heinrich Hoffmann

As he trudg'd along to school,
It was always Johnny's rule
To be looking at the sky
And the clouds that floated by;
But what just before him lay,
in his way,
Johnny never thought about;
So that everyone cried out—
"Look at little John there,
Little Johnny Head-in-Air!"
Running just in Johnny's way,
Came a little dog one day;
Johnny's eyes were still astray
Up on high,
In the sky;
And he never heard them cry—
"Johnny, mind, the dog is nigh!"
Bump!
Dump!
Down they fall, with such a thump,
Dog and Johnny in a lump!
Once, with head as high as ever,
Johnny walk'd beside the river.
Johnny watch'd the swallows trying
Which was cleverest at flying.
Oh! What fun!
Johnny watch'd the bright round sun
Going in and coming out;
This was all he thought about.
To the river's very brink,
Where the bank was high and steep,

And the water very deep;
And the fishes, in a row,
Started to see him coming so.

One step more! Oh! Sad to tell!
Headlong in poor Johnny fell.
And the fishes, in dismay,
Wagg'd their tails and ran away.
There lay Johnny on his face,
With his nice red writing-case;
But, as they were passing by,
Two strong men had heard him cry;
And, with sticks, these two strong men
Hook'd poor Johnny out again.

Oh! You should have seen him shiver
When they pull'd him from the river
He was in a sorry plight!
Dripping wet, and such a fright!
Wet all over, everywhere,
Clothes, and arms, and face, and hair.
Johnny never will forget
What it is to be so wet.

And the fishes, one, two, three,
Are come back again, you see;
Up they came the moment after,
To enjoy the fun and laughter.
Each popp'd out his little head,
And, to tease poor Johnny said:
"Silly little Johnny, look,
You have lost your writing-book!"

Hoffmann did not put a name on what he was describing. Any teacher or parent who has dealt with children with ADHD, with or without hyperactivity, can see these children in Hoffmann's descriptions.

The first apparent documentation of the disorder appeared in 1902 when Dr. George Frederic Still, a British physician, described a group of twenty children who displayed what he called *moral control defects*. These children were impulsive, aggressive, defiant, prone to accidents, and seemed unable to control their behaviors. Previously, such children were considered to be the result of bad parenting. What Still noticed, however, was that these children all had what seemed to be good parents. Dr. Still apparently was the first to suggest that the problem was one of biology rather than one of poor parenting.

An encephalitis epidemic during 1917–1918 further supported Still's suggestion. Doctors studying a group of encephalitis survivors who had suffered brain damage noticed that they had behaviors similar to Dr. Still's group including inattention, poor impulse control, and overactivity. They made the connection between ADHD–type behaviors and the organic brain damage they had suffered.

In 1937, another link was forged to the biological cause of ADHD–type behaviors when Charles Bradley began using stimulants to successfully treat poor attention, overactivity, and impulsivity. Soon the term *minimal brain dysfunction* began to be used to describe those who exhibited such behaviors.

By 1957, the collection of symptoms was called the *hyperkinetic syndrome* and brain research was being conducted to find a specific area of the brain that might be the cause. In 1968, the syndrome appeared for the first time in Second Edition of the *Diagnostic and Statistical Manual of Mental Disorders (DSM)*—the standard classification resource used by mental health workers, and was called *Hyperkinetic Reaction of Childhood*. The attempt at finding a specific brain dysfunction continued to be a focus of research throughout the 1960s, centering primarily on the hyperactivity of children.

During the 1970s, researchers and educators began to see lack of attention and impulse control as larger problems than hyperactivity, so the focus of research shifted. When *DSM-III* was published in 1980, these new understandings were evident. The previous category, Hyperkinetic Reaction of Childhood, was divided into two categories: Attention-Deficit Disorder with Hyperactivity and Attention-Deficit Disorder without Hyperactivity. The revised edition of *DSM-III* further differentiated the terms as Attention-Deficit Hyperactivity Disorder and Undifferentiated Attention-Deficit Disorder.

The latest major revision of *DSM* was in 1994 *(DSM-IV)* with a text revision in July 2000 *(DSM-IV-TR)*. The disorder has again taken on a new name and new categories with three diagnoses available for physicians: Attention-Deficit/Hyperactivity Disorder–Predominantly Inattentive Type, Attention-Deficit/Hyperactivity Disorder–Predominantly Hyperactive-Impulsive Type, and Attention-Deficit/Hyperactivity Disorder–Combined Type (see Figure 2–1).

Attention-Deficit/Hyperactivity Disorder Criteria

A. Either (1) or (2)

(1) six (or more) of the following symptoms of **inattention** have persisted for at least six months to a degree that is maladaptive and inconsistent with developmental level.

Inattention

(a) often fails to give close attention to details or makes careless mistakes in schoolwork, work, or other activities

(b) often has difficulty sustaining attention in tasks or play activities

(c) often does not seem to listen when spoken to directly

(d) often does not follow through on instructions and fails to finish schoolwork, chores, or duties in the workplace (not due to oppositional behavior or failure to understand instructions)

(e) often has difficulty organizing tasks and activities

(f) often avoids, dislikes, or is reluctant to engage in tasks that require sustained mental effort (such as schoolwork or homework)

(g) often loses things necessary for tasks or activities (e.g., toys, school assignments, pencils, books, or tools)

(h) is often easily distracted by extraneous stimuli

(i) is often forgetful in daily activities

(2) six (or more) of the following symptoms of **hyperactivity-impulsivity** have persisted for at least six months to a degree that is maladaptive and inconsistent with developmental level.

Hyperactivity

(a) often fidgets with hands or feet or squirms in seat

(b) often leaves seat in classroom or in other situations in which remaining seated is expected

(c) often runs about or climbs excessively in situations in which it is inappropriate (in adolescents or adults, may be limited to subjective feelings of restlessness)

(d) often has difficulty playing or engaging in leisure activities quietly

(e) is often "on the go" or often acts as if "driven by a motor"

(f) often talks excessively

Figure 2–1 Diagnostic Criteria for Attention-Deficit Disorders from DSM-IV-TR

Attention-Deficit/Hyperactivity Disorder Criteria

Impulsivity

    (g) often blurts out answers before questions have been completed

    (h) often has difficulty awaiting turn

    (i) often interrupts or intrudes on others (e.g., butts into conversations or games)

B. Some hyperactive-impulsive or inattentive symptoms that caused impairment were present before age 7 years.

C. Some impairment from the symptoms is present in two or more settings (e.g., at school [or work] and at home).

D. There must be clear evidence of clinically significant impairment in social, academic, or occupational functioning.

E. The symptoms do not occur exclusively during the course of a Pervasive Developmental Disorder, Schizophrenia, or other Psychotic Disorder and are not better accounted for by another mental disorder (e.g., Mood Disorder, Anxiety Disorder, Dissociative Disorder, or a Personality Disorder).

Specify Type

♦ Attention-Deficit/Hyperactivity Disorder–Combined Type: If both Criteria A1 and A2 are met for the past six months

♦ Attention-Deficit/Hyperactivity Disorder–Predominantly Inattentive Type: If Criterion A1 is met but Criterion A2 is not met for the past six months

♦ Attention-Deficit/Hyperactivity Disorder–Predominantly Hyperactive-Impulsive Type: If Criterion A2 is met but Criterion A1 is not met for the past six months

Figure 2–1 Diagnostic Criteria for Attention-Deficit Disorders from DSM-IV-TR, *(cont.). Reprinted with permission from the* Diagnostic and Statistical Manual of Mental Disorders, *Fourth Edition, Text Revision. Copyright 2000, American Psychiatric Association.*

What Is ADHD?

ADHD is perhaps the most widely studied childhood psychiatric disorder. Researchers continue to look for causes: Is it neurological? Is it caused by a chemical imbalance? Are neurotransmitters to blame? Research has resulted in deeper understandings by teachers, doctors, parents, and students, leading to more astute and accurate diagnoses and attempts at more appropriate remediation. Yet, all these attempts by the medical field to define and describe this disorder are only helpful if they translate into an ability to understand those who live with it every day.

What is ADHD? The *DSM-IV-TR* describes it, but it is the voices of those who wake up and struggle with it every day who can help you understand it. Listen to their voices.

Jillian

"It's a different way of thinking. It's not being able to focus. Not knowing how to focus but knowing that you should and trying to. Then you're completely lost in the fact that you had to focus to begin with and you're in a state of confusion. You don't know how to say something. You have it on the tip of your tongue but you can't say it. You think of it but it comes out all wrong.

"It's a different way of learning. Having homework and not being able to focus because these papers aren't correct, my pen's over there, I have to turn the lights out, I have to go do this, I have to fidget and do a dance before I can sit down and study.

"It's a completely different outlook on life, a personality characteristic. Just listen to my conversation. I've been babbling about things for a half hour and I don't even realize what I'm talking about. It's like that except all the time, every year."

Jennie

"It's concentrating on everything at once. Hearing everything, knowing everything, seeing everything.

"You walk into the grocery store and look in your pocketbook. No list. What do you need? You start walking around the store. 'This looks good, this looks good, this looks good.' Before you know it, you're buying tons of stuff and your cart is full. You have not bought anything that you know is on your list. What do you do? You go back throughout the store. You still grab a bunch of stuff you don't want. You're walking around and you finally remember a few things and you put them in your basket. You check out only to realize after you get out of the store that you forgot six or seven things so you go all the way back in and you get all those things and you walk all the way back out. I'll go home and say to myself, 'Why did I buy all this stuff?' Oh yeah, because I couldn't remember my list.

"That's what ADD is, this constant 'everything happening at once,' all these impulses around you and you're constantly paying attention to them. Because you're paying attention to all this food and all your impulses, you don't remember all the stuff you were supposed to do because you forgot the list which was supposed to help you but it isn't with you.

"That's what ADD is, it's all these impulses. Boom, boom boom. I need this, I need that. Let me pay attention to this and that and this and that and this and that. You're thinking so much that you lose sight of what you're supposed to be focusing on, whether it be the professor, or the list, or whatever. Everything's coming at you—all this food, tons of food everywhere. It's like, take it all and then forget the one thing that you actually need or the one person you're supposed to be listening to. That's my analogy."

Nick

"I describe it as just having trouble finding an interest in things and having trouble focusing on things that aren't of interest. When it comes to things I'm interested in, I don't have any problems focusing, especially athletics. I don't have any problem focusing on any part of it, whether it's the actual event or whether it's the strategy behind it. I can focus on it and I can remember things like stats and stuff like that. But when it comes to typical things, books and things that you really need to learn, I think it's just harder for kids with ADD to bring themselves to enjoy something that maybe they don't understand or it's just something that doesn't seem to interest them right away."

Jessie

"We're not stupid. We're not troublemakers. It's not that we don't care about stuff. It's that we want to take the path of visiting all the cool things and looking at all the interesting stuff and seeking out ways to fulfill an interest and excite us. There's a mental block almost to doing stuff that is not interesting and stuff that does not make us happy, stuff that does not feel fulfilling."

Grant

"I think of it as several different ways to think or to go about solving a problem. The way that I think of it in my head is that there is point A and point B and most people think of how to get from point A to point B by just going straight, [but] people with ADD will kind of go around and visit C first and then D as long as they get to B sometime. That's kind of the way I think of it."

Jill

"I think it is different for everyone who has it. With me, it's just like I'll be sitting there doing something and I will click off and go to something else. I know that when I am sitting down I will have to do my thing for a half an hour. Then I am going to do something else and then come back and do this. And it's with anything, not only schoolwork. I can only clean for half an hour. I can only spend a certain amount of time doing only one thing. I just get bored and frustrated with it. The way my mind works is that I will be talking with someone and oh and then and I want to do this and that and blah, blah, blah. I'm all over the place like a Ping-Pong ball shooting everywhere."

Geoff

"It's the tendency to lose focus, to not stay focused. Not being able to stay in tune with what I'm reading. I know it has an effect on everything. What I think is wrong with me is even getting distracted from everyday things. It's something that I do for myself in everyday things. I'll distract myself like it's a reflex or something like that."

Travis

"I would look at the blackboard and think hard about what corrections I needed to make, but while I'm still looking straight ahead, a laser show starts in my head. First a beam shoots in from one side and then another and before you know it, I'm just sitting back watching the show instead of doing my work." (Travis' mother told me this story one night over dinner. This was his explanation of why he wasn't getting work done at school.)

Rob at Fourteen

"It's when there are so many things going on around you, you have to go do one of those things and when you get there you do something else, completely forgetting your last thing. For me, sitting in class and trying to pay attention to the teacher when someone is tapping a pencil is impossible. When I'm supposed to be doing my homework and the fan is moving, I have to turn off the fan before I can do the work. And when I get up to turn off the fan, the cat is lying on the floor and I have to pet the cat. When I'm down on the floor with the cat and I see a ball ten feet away, I get up and start playing with the ball. That's what ADD is."

Rob at Eighteen

"ADHD is not necessarily the inability to focus. It's the inability to not focus on everything. The problem is I focus on everything and I can't not focus on everything. I was sitting in the room with a bunch of people. There were three conversations going on and I was listening to them all. It was confusing to me because I was listening to three conversations and I couldn't understand any of them.

"If the teacher was trying to teach a lesson and the two kids behind me were passing notes and the kid next to me was tapping his pencil, I would be paying attention to each one of those things. Because I was paying attention to all of them, I couldn't fully understand what the teacher was saying. The problem comes in when I'm doing homework and I'm paying attention to that and three other things. No matter what those three other things are, they're much more interesting than my homework.

"I just figured out what ADD is. I'm sitting here listening to you and my mind will start going on a train of thought and you don't know you're on this train of thought until you realize you're not listening."

This neurological disorder that's called ADHD is all of the following. In a structured, organized culture filled with structured, organized schools that emphasize time, obedience, and a finished product, it is also much, much more.

What Is ADHD?

◆ A neurological dysfunction characterized by inattention, overactivity, and impulsivity

◆ A mental block

◆ A different way of thinking and learning

◆ The inability not to focus on everything

◆ The inability to focus if it's not interesting

◆ Everything coming at you

◆ A struggle with organization

◆ Too much information and too many thoughts

◆ A state of confusion

♦ All these impulses—boom, boom, boom

♦ Babbling conversation

♦ Turn off the fan, no, play with the cat, no, play with the ball

♦ A forgotten grocery list

♦ Visiting all the cool things

♦ A path that detours on its way to the goal

♦ A laser light show

♦ A Ping-Pong ball

Is ADHD for real? Jill invites you to "come live in my world and you'll see how it is." Ask Jennie that question and she'll tell you, "If it doesn't exist, I would like to know why I'm like this. If people could spend one day with my brain, they would die. Just spend one day in my head and you will cry yourself to sleep that night. I wish it didn't exist."

In all its complexity and amidst all the confusion, Attention-Deficit/Hyperactivity Disorder does exist. For ten to twenty-five million people, it is very, very real.

Jennie's Story
Half Off in the Middle of Nowhere, Always

My mom asked me how I would describe ADHD. There's kind of an iron circle around you, like a cage they keep birds in. That's what I feel like. I'm cramped into something and I can't move.

Symptoms and Diagnosis

When I was a kid, everything in my room was pushed against the wall with a huge space in the middle because I would just bounce on everything. I was always moving. My mother always said, "You don't walk. You bounce."

When I came home from school she would put on loud, annoying, obnoxious, kid music and I would just bounce—literally, hopping up and down, around the room. I would bounce and scream, jump off the coffee tables and the couches and bop on everything. She would just let me go. "If that's what you have to do, then you have to do it," she said, "You would get on the coffee table and you would jump onto the couch. Then you would jump onto the other one and you'd jump on the floor. Then you'd start all over again. You would bounce everywhere."

I was always the kid who was up the earliest. I hardly ever slept. My mother never got any sleep. I would go to bed at one in the morning because I couldn't sleep and I'd get up at 5 or 6 A.M. My mom used to say to me, "You were always up at the crack of dawn even on the weekends. At first I wanted to shoot myself but later I said, 'Forget it.' I'd get up with you and lie on the couch in my pajamas and watch you bound around while I tried to half sleep half stay awake and keep an eye on you. I gave up trying to get up with you because I couldn't. You just got to go with it."

My mom has ADD too, really bad. She won't admit it. They never tested her but you can definitely tell. You'd be talking to her and she would say, "Sorry, what did you just say?" And my sister has it too. I don't know how my mom survived me and now she gets my sister. I think that she's just so out of it too.

We never had a clean home—ever. It was always messy. When I was a kid my mom said she never had anything expensive because I'd always break it. "You never meant to but you always did." Once I came home from school and said, "I got a good grade on my test." I ran to the couch and threw myself on it, jumping up and down. The couch tipped over and I heard a crash. My mom said, "That's OK. Let's go out to eat. Let's go celebrate." She didn't even look at the statue that broke. She just said, "Where do you want to go?"

I was never on time to anything. I'm still never on time. I have my watch set for five minutes ahead because if I don't, I'm late to everything. I'm always late because I get so involved in something and I completely lose track of time. That always happens to me.

People say that's not ADD, that's inability to be on time. They don't understand. I'm doing something and I get so involved in it, the world does not exist. Just that one little thing. Everything else disappears. I can't bring myself away from it. That's a form of ADD. Usually I focus on everything but sometimes I focus on one thing and it's horrible. Sometimes I get stuck on that one thing and forget about everything else. That used to happen to me all the time. My friends always called me the space cadet.

I write big and I write fast. It's illegible because I'm thinking so fast. I never ever got a good grade on handwriting—"Needs improvement. Please practice at home." Illegible, always. I had teachers in high school who said, "If you don't type it, I won't accept it because I won't be able to read it." I always felt so bad.

In high school English we had these freewrite things where we had to write for ten minutes nonstop. My teacher looked at me once and asked, "What is that supposed to say?" I said, "I wrote five pages." And he said, "But they're lines." I said, "No, they're not. They're letters. Some of them just didn't get formed completely."

Elementary School

They thought I had a reading problem in the first grade because when I get nervous I shut down. I was in the highest reading group and someone made fun of me, so I just stopped talking. They brought me down to the middle reading group, which I didn't really like. It was too easy for me. I got really quiet, very shy. I thought I was stupid.

In second grade, they brought me down to the lowest reading group and gave me an extra reading class, which meant I missed math and everything else you miss at the beginning of second grade. I missed word problems, which I still can't do today. My mom asked why I had to miss math. "Anything else but math. Anything. Even reading. She doesn't need two readings." And they said, "No, that's when the reading group is."

Finally, in fifth grade they took me out of the reading group. I was in this reading group all these years and it wasn't doing anything. I was fine in reading. I just got shy and didn't want to talk. And then before I knew it, I got stuck in the lowest math group because I wasn't in math to learn all the math, so I didn't know any of the math. It was like a never-ending cycle. And so I had all these problems and of course bouncing up and down, ADDing and everything else.

Third grade I always lost my papers. We'd have a worksheet and we couldn't bring the book home, only the worksheet. To get a paper of mine from school to home was an impossible task for me to do. My mother would search my bag for it. She'd drive me back to school and we used to search my desk—never find it. All I could think of was maybe it was on the bus. We never found papers. My teacher used to get so frustrated with me in third grade. She never showed it, but I knew. She was annoyed but she never actually said anything. She'd just hand me another piece of paper. That one would get lost too. She never flunked me or anything but she was never too happy.

Here is a humiliating story. I was so depressed when this happened. This [was in] the third-grade math class. We used to switch for math and my teacher said we had to have a paper done by the end of the day and pass it back in to her. I panicked. "Gotta do it." So I did it right away while we were having a test in English class. During that, I'm doing my math work. I'm so paranoid; I had to get this paper done. Needless to say, I flunked the test. I didn't do anything on the test. I was so upset. I came home crying. I found out at the end of the day that we could take home the math paper and hand it in the next day if we wanted to.

The teacher should have noticed during the test that I was doing my math work and stopped me, or noticed the test at the end and said, "Jennie, why didn't you do your work?" If it had been me, I would have said, "OK, stay after school and we'll do the test." Why flunk a person just because they got so intent on something else? It's not my fault. It's not that I didn't know the stuff.

The Yellow Paper

Then I got to fourth grade, which was the year from hell. Basically, I was just stuck in a rut—low math group, low reading group that I felt uncomfortable in because I felt I could do better than that.

Then there was the whole math paper situation. We had to use the yellow math paper. God forbid if you don't have the right paper for math. I had that happen so many times when I was in fourth grade. The teacher used to have this yellow paper and you were supposed to get it before the end of the day, that one piece of yellow math paper. Did I ever remember the yellow math paper? If by chance I remembered it, I usually messed it up to the point that it was illegible. I had to erase and it would rip. I would put it on notebook paper, and she would never accept it if it was on notebook paper. I took one [sheet of] paper to do the whole entire problem. I write huge.

It got to the point where my mother used to write to school: "Jennie is incapable of doing her math the first time. Unless you want her to copy it onto this paper, it probably is not going to come to school on this paper." It was just bad. She said to the teacher, "You don't understand. She sits down and she does her work and she gets frustrated or goes off in her own little world or whatever." Before I know it I screw up the whole paper or I'm erasing until there are holes in it. What is the big deal with notebook paper or yellow paper? The teacher said, "If it's not on yellow paper she gets a zero." I always forgot the yellow paper. My mother hunted for it too but you can't buy it in the store. I asked the teacher, "Can I have a stack to take home or a bunch or could I have more than one piece?" She replied, "No, only one piece of the yellow paper." So my mother would make me write my homework on a notebook paper and then copy it over. It was still messy.

We had morning work on the board and that was on little gray paper, not yellow paper. There was a student teacher that year too. She felt so bad for me that she would sneak me extra paper.

The fourth-grade teacher hated me. I could not sit in my seat. I was always bouncing up and down. She was one of those teachers where you're in rows—you don't move, you sit there the whole day and I'm like bouncing everywhere, clicking my glasses case, opening and closing it. She would say, "Will you stop." I couldn't help it.

I'd come home and bounce off the walls. My mom would say, "Jennie, what's wrong with you? What did they do, give you ten pounds of sugar in school?" What's wrong with me? One day she came to school and sat in the classroom and she's like, "You don't move all day. No wonder you act like that at home." That was the first year they had bathrooms outside the class, which was like a blessing to me. I used to ask to go to the bathroom so many times because I had to move.

I don't remember doing projects in her class. I remember homework. Anytime you didn't have it exactly the way she wanted it, it was a zero. It wasn't whether it was right or wrong, it was just a zero.

I remember in fourth grade I flunked the California Tests so badly because we had to sit there and take them all day long. I just couldn't take it. You don't understand, I just had to move. "No, you can't go anywhere." But I wanted to move. I couldn't concentrate because I was so intent on moving and getting up and not sitting there. I didn't want to be there and I just couldn't concentrate.

Finally Someone Listens to Me

I really liked my fifth-grade teacher. The first day of school she's watching me, keeping an eye on me and helping me out. Right off the bat she started giving me strategies like, "Jennie, if you keep your notes kind of organized, even if you're not organized yourself, if you try to keep them organized and make an effort at the end of the day to clean your desk, you'll be able to find things easier."

I thought, "Oh, what a concept." So about five minutes before the day ended she would say, "Jen" and I would empty everything out of my desk. I'd put everything back in somewhat more organized. There I was sitting on the floor, books on the chair—I was quite the sight.

I think the fourth-grade teacher pulled her aside and said, "She never does homework on the right paper." So the fifth-grade teacher gave me a package of each type of paper and said, "You will always have paper. If you run out, tell me and I'll get you more." She was awesome. She had me get organized for the most part with my desk.

She realized I was in the lowest reading and math group. She's the one who realized I should probably go up a little bit so she put me in the middle group and moved me up slowly. She was the reading and math teacher for the middle groups so she felt more comfortable with me being there. She was just really great. Finally, somebody was listening to me. It was wonderful.

I did a lot better in fifth grade. My teacher was really big on projects and I love projects. She was funny and she got me organized.

I was the only kid in class with a special homework folder and the only thing that went in that folder was homework. It had an "in"and an "out" side. It never left my bag. I had to take my papers up to my bag and put them in it. The folder didn't come. I'd take the papers from the bag and leave the folder in there and that way I'd never lose it.

The teacher used to call me in the morning and say, "Do you have this book? And this book? Do you have this homework?" Sometimes she'd call at night when we had projects and say, "Your project is coming up at the end of the week. Make sure you have this, this, and this." And the night before, she'd call me and say, "Do you have all your posters?" She was really good about that and she didn't have to be. She didn't have to call me but she did.

Once I didn't have a project done on time. I had nothing. I was so flustered and I was crying. She said, "Calm down. There is tomorrow." I said, "But it's due today." She said, "Yes, but it's not done. There is tomorrow, but no later than tomorrow. So what are you going to do when you go home today?" I said, "Finish it." That meant a lot to me because I was so hysterical that I had completely forgotten it. It was a Monday. I do not do well on Monday. I think she knew that. She said, "I knew that I shouldn't have given you that on Monday. We'll have to chalk it up to both of our mistakes. We both should have realized that Mondays are bad for you but tomorrow is another day." I really appreciated that.

When I look at my students I think I'll do the same thing. Sometimes stuff happens. A lot of teachers really don't think of that. What if your dog died over the weekend and you really couldn't do it? You were too depressed. Mine was just that I completely forgot. But that meant a lot to me. Maybe when you get to high school it wouldn't be a good idea because kids would walk all over you. But I think in fourth or fifth grade, kids don't know enough to take advantage of it. They think, "Thank God, you're really nice."

Middle and High School: Half Off in the Middle of Nowhere, Always

In tenth grade, I had a teacher who had fifty-point multiple-choice and fifty-point essay tests. Can Jen do that in fifty minutes? No. He used to have the attitude of, "Go through the multiple choice and guess if you have to because the essay is the most important." But to me, it was only 50 points and I was so hung up on the multiple choice, which I usually do first anyway because I feel better about that. He would not give us longer. I hated that class. I never did good on his tests and he had the attitude of "Well, you obviously don't belong here. This is the honors-level class and you don't deserve it. You need to be in level two, college level." I was just so hurt by that.

I was diagnosed with ADHD in high school. I think I was the one that said something. "You know, something's wrong with me because I can't concentrate in class." I spaced out all the time in class. I realized I had trouble sitting still. I had never heard of ADD at that point. I just said to my doctor once, "Is something wrong with me? Do I have a sugar deficiency or excessive? I can never sit still and I have trouble concentrating."

The doctor started talking to me and at some point started talking to my teachers and came up with it. They gave me an IQ test and compared that to what I was actually doing in school.

High school was a challenge. I was always rushing to every class and a lot of the teachers hated when I was late. I was always late.

I was always half off in the middle of nowhere, always. Never having work done. If I did it, it was always at least a day late. I was horrible about that. It wasn't even that I didn't do it. It was just that I didn't remember to bring it in. I always forgot it on the kitchen table—never failed. Freshman year, people were really liberal about it. Sophomore year, it was like, "If it's not here today, it's a zero." "It's on the kitchen table," I'd say. They wouldn't let you call your home. My mom was always so willing to run it into school but they would never let you call.

In sophomore year nobody really cared about your well-being. They just seemed so inflexible. It wasn't junior year where you were getting stuff out of classes and it wasn't senior year where you were doing college stuff. You were just a lonely, little sophomore. So I just slipped right under and nobody even really caught it. I think I played sick more times that school year than I've ever been sick from school in my life. I didn't want to go to school, didn't want to do my work. It got to the point where I started slacking off and I'd do some of the work but not all. I'd look at my friends' papers instead of doing my own homework.

My health teacher was awesome. She realized almost immediately that I was unhappy and she switched me into her other class. She put me in a class with my friends and I felt so much better. I actually did good in her class because of that. It was like she noticed; she cared. She didn't just think I was moping around for nothing.

I felt like they didn't pay any attention to what their students were capable of or needed. It's just so easy to slip through the cracks when you're not being challenged. If they expect you to only do this much work, you're only going to do this much work. If they expect you to do a lot of work, you're probably going to work to achieve as close to that as possible. Maybe you won't but you're more likely to. You'll at least go above the lower level than if they just gave you bare minimum work. I just felt like they didn't care and it was a joke. It didn't help matters that I spaced out all the time in class.

Making It in College Where People Actually Care

In college it was different; teachers were different. I felt that people were friendlier. My psych teacher realized I had ADD and she was like, "Oh, my gosh, you are too funny. You have ADD don't you?" She just thought I was the cutest thing. I just talked the whole class through. I never shut up. I was just so hyper. It was about ten in the morning and I was probably bouncing.

One of my professors used to be a seventh-grade teacher and she was just so nice. She did lots of projects. She really cared about our learning and what we had learned in the past. It was good to know there wasn't one right way like it used to be.

My English teacher, at first I thought, "I'm going to hate this guy." He walks into class and says, "Who wants to drop? This class is too full." I'm like, hide me. I guess what it turned out to be is that he just wanted a small class. One of the things he said to us is, "English is your language. Learn how to use it. I won't accept papers that aren't perfect." I'm like, "I'm going to cry." But then I really started to like him. He really had this attitude that you're going to make an effort. It's not an option. You're going to fail if you don't make an effort. That to me was awesome and amazing and wonderful because I was like, finally, someone who cares. Someone who wants us to succeed. I was making a strong effort because if he wanted me to, then I wanted to. I wanted to get a good grade. I didn't want to fail the class. He never gave you a grade before he had conferences with you. He'd tell you what was wrong with the paper.

He yelled at me once for using the word "for" in place of "because." He thought it didn't sound right. I'm rebellious and I kept it in anyway. He circled it in big red marker and said, "I told you to take this out. I think you're just being stubborn." He gave me a really good grade on that paper. He said, "I probably would have given you a B or something but when I saw that, I thought, 'She has control over her own writing.'" It made me feel good. Somebody who respected the fact that I had an opinion. My work was important to me and I had pride and ownership in my paper now. I didn't just go with what he told me to like I probably would have done in high school. Slowly but surely I own something.

I'm really good at portfolios because I can organize them really neat. Once I get started there's no stopping. I have to go straight through. Most people do it in chunks. If I did it in chunks, it would look so choppy you could tell. I just do it straight through. People say, "You've got to be out of your mind." And I say, "No, trust me. Twenty four hours I'll be done." I just do it and they come out fine. I work so amazingly well under pressure. I just can't do things in chunks. That's just me. I have to just sit down a day or two before and get it over with.

In college I've doubled my GPA. Last semester I got straight As. I think all the professors are much more understanding. Sometimes you have a better advantage of succeeding because people actually care. They are willing to accommodate and help out and actually care about their students. I care about learning because my professors care about it.

I'm sure some of my high school teachers cared. My sophomore year was just so bad that I think from that point on I gave up and I didn't care anymore. That's all there was to it, and it was downhill for me.

Staying Focused

One of the things one of my professors did was write the topics on the board and I would wait for him to bring up all those topics. I would listen for just that topic and if he would go off on tangents, I would lose him because I was waiting for that one topic. If he would say something, I would look in the book because I would want to see more about it—I would be looking for the chapter on it. He would keep going and I would want to stay on it; I would want to read more about it in the book. I'd say to myself, "Don't do that because you'll miss what he's saying." It's horrible.

I can stay on topic. But if I don't, I'm off completely. I will either stick with one thing he's saying, or something else will catch my attention, or I'll be staring at somebody else or out the window. Or I'll be watching the clock or something happens and I lose it.

When I read, I have to run the pencil or my finger down the page or off I go. I have to stay on focus. That's what I have to do. I have to be doing something to keep myself there. Last night I was reading *Harry Potter* and before I knew it I was staring off into space. Half hour later, "Oh, I was reading." It's horrible. It's getting worse.

People see my textbooks and ask, "Why is everything under-lined?" I just keep on underlining as I go along. It's not for impor-tant stuff. It's so I stay on-task. It's tactile. It's another sense I can use to keep myself focused. Everything's underlined. It's gotten to the point where I even underline leisure reading because it helps me stay on-task.

That's another reason why high school was such a challenge to read textbooks. I couldn't underline so I would run my finger and I would lose it even more. I can't tell you how many erasers I went through erasing my underlines.

I still count on my fingers. People say, "Oh, you can't count." I can. I can, it's just that if I do that I can stay focused.

Getting Organized

When I left high school I was the biggest slob. It was horrible. When I got to college, I had to share a room with someone so I knew that I should be neat. Basically everything had its place and it didn't move from its place. I just picked a spot where something was going to be. The first day my mom said, "Don't ever move it and if you do, put it back where you found it and that way you'll never lose anything." Oh, what a concept. I did that and it became an obsession because if some-one moved something I noticed.

All my books are on my bookshelf by size not by class; my fold-ers and binders are all there. I was going to do it by class but then it got really messy because some of the books are paperbacks. Then I have a little plastic thing my mother bought me and I put paper in it. The bottom little drawer in the plastic thing is my paper clips and in the first drawer in my desk, always, are my pencils and pens. In the second drawer is construction paper and stuff and in the bottom drawer I keep computer stuff that I might need and my portfolios. And I have a drawer that is my junk drawer. That's how I do it. I limit myself to what I have to, to bare essentials. Pens and pencils are a huge big thing. But I just try to have as little as possible. And I just try to keep them so they're always on my desk.

Usually I'm not as organized as I should be. Basically it's like, things have a place, but they don't always go there for a day or two. Usually when I see the pile on my desk, I'll say, "Oh, I need to get rid of that pile" and I'll put everything back where it goes. It usu-ally stays there for a day. It usually ends up on my bed, then goes on the floor.

Lots of Notes

I have Post-it notes everywhere. I always have lists of things I need to do. I'm always copying over a list. I can't stand a messy list. Homework is a separate list and that is by class. I have my other list of things to do and I will keep eight million copies everywhere and paste [them] everywhere. If I have anything important to do it goes right on the calendar. I have a huge calendar and everything is on there. If it isn't on there, it doesn't exist. People don't believe me. They don't understand. If it's not on that calendar, it could be in my assignment notebook, it could be on my whiteboard, it could be flashing on my computer screen. If it's not on that calendar, it doesn't happen. It doesn't exist. I would just completely forget about it. It has to be there. It's the only way that I can tell when things are supposed to happen.

I don't put homework on the calendar. I probably should. With homework, that's the hardest thing for me. I can't tell you how many chapters I am supposed to have read for certain classes that I never read. I'm always cramming when it comes to tests. I always forget to read things.

Always Losing Things

I lose everything. It's horrible. I try to do homework in my room so I don't lose it. There's a couch seat right when you walk in the door and so much of my stuff goes there, the bag and everything. I'm running around, "Has anybody seen my bookbag?" It's worse than living at home. I'm always losing everything. We have so many closets. I never remember what goes in which closet. There's more than one bathroom. I have all my bathroom stuff in a bucket that stays in the back bathroom. The front bathroom has the shower and all my stuff for the shower is there.

Last night I spent about ten minutes banging on my own door because everyone went to bed and I had no keys. I proceeded to search the entire apartment and found them in this coat. It was on the floor in my room because I had a different coat on. I have a front closet where we keep all of our coats so I also lose coats quickly because there always [are other] coats there. I always wear another one. I do have a little hook that my keys go on right when you walk in the room. I say "hook, hook, hook" while I'm walking toward it. That's the first thing I try to do. If I don't have to unlock the door, I completely forget that they're in my pocket. I won't even think. They end up in the pocket and then that's not the coat that I have on.

Medication

I started taking Ritalin in college. I only take it for classes. In history class I would die without it. I went one time without it and I had to get the notes from the professor. I had absolutely nothing. He said, "You usually have ten pages of notes. What were you doing the whole time?"

I said, "Making a grocery list and trying to remember what I'm supposed to do next. I did however catch something about the New Deal, but only a couple of words." He basically gave me his lecture notes. I knew I was forgetting something that morning.

The thing I find humorous is that attention deficit kids tend to have a lot of trouble remembering things. When they do, they give them a pill every four hours to help them remember. It doesn't work that well. I never did remember to take the pill. I carried some in my bag so if I remembered I could take it then.

When I take Ritalin, I can focus clearer. I can focus really well. But the thing is, God forbid someone would say something that would catch my attention and then I'm stuck on that for an hour. It helps you focus but you've got to make sure that your attention goes to the right thing because if it doesn't, you're so going to be stuck on something else.

I feel like when I take it I focus in so tight on one thing that nothing else is in my view. If you can get focused on the right thing, you're golden. But if you can't, you're so in trouble because you don't see anything else. It's almost worse sometimes than not being on it. If you can get that right thing, you're fine.

If a child would really benefit from medication, don't deprive the child of it. At the same time, don't think it's the answer or the only option.

Closing Thoughts

I think the real world is what people with ADHD are going to make of it. Just because they have a roundabout engaged way of doing things doesn't mean that they're going to be destroyed for life, that they're never going to be able to do structured stuff. I think, as you get older you're more capable of doing structured stuff than when you're young. I think little by little they're going to be able to do more, but you know what? Who cares if they're not going to be structured?

People who are flighty and off the wall make the best artists. You may think they're absolutely out of their minds but they're like some of the best people you'll ever meet. So what if they're a little flighty and off the wall. I think people like that are great. There's nothing wrong with that.

People ask me, "If you could choose not to have ADD, would you?" No, there's way too much I can do all at once. I may be a space cadet but I can multitask like you can't even imagine. My mother thinks it's funny. One time she came in the kitchen and I was talking on the computer with my friend, stirring soup, helping my sister with her homework, talking on the phone and my mom says, "You give me a headache just looking at you." I don't even realize it because with ADD you can just focus on everything and do everything at once or you can just obsessively focus on one teeny tiny little thing that no one else can even notice. It's like you never know which one you're going to be doing.

I still struggle to get through some days. There are always easy days and there will always be hard days. But I survive with my big calendar and color-coding. What can I say? We all have obstacles to overcome. Mine just isn't that obvious or viewable.

Symptoms of ADHD
I See It All, I Hear It All

You've had them in your classroom—those students who often-times defy description. You want to understand them. You try every-thing you know to help them. Sometimes you're successful but more often than not you come home frustrated. That's exactly how the students feel.

Don't get discouraged. Attention Deficit/Hyperactivity Disorder (ADHD) is a complex diagnosis with diverse symptoms. It is a med-ical diagnosis with the primary characteristics being inattention, impulsivity, and overactivity. The diagnosis, with its representative symptoms, translates into behaviors; those behaviors impact routine daily activities, social interactions, and schooling. Often the diagno-sis comes as a result of the inability to function in schools as they are structured today. When tasks require compliance, timelines, obedi-ence, and uniformity, the child who often seems to be marching to the beat of a different drummer is likely to struggle.

Most people will have some ADHD symptoms at one time or another. Sometimes they forget lists or homework, lose track of what someone is saying, or forget a name. The difference for those with ADHD is that the symptoms are persistent and pervasive, seriously impacting their ability to function successfully. What makes those challenged with ADHD unique is that, as Jillian described it, "It's like that except all the time and every year."

The symptoms are diverse. For the storytellers, the only constant was that they were not doing as well in school as teachers and parents thought they could. Most of them felt that something was just not right—something was different about them.

The *DSM-IV-TR* criteria (see Figure 2–1) only tell part of the story. These criteria can be broken down into a multitude of behavioral characteristics—diverse and complex. Yet even a description of these characteristics is artificial; the storytellers are more than the individ-ual behaviors they exhibit. If, however, the symptoms can be identi-fied for what they are, perhaps you can begin to understand the life of a child challenged with ADHD and begin to create an environment that does make sense. It is the totality of the children's experiences that makes teachers' understanding so much greater.

Kristina's Story

Her mom was the first to begin to put the pieces of Kristina's puzzle together. "Reading was where I saw the first sign. I'd sit down and read with her and she would just stumble over so many words. Her first grade teacher had noted that she thought that she had reading problems and to watch her carefully." She had been reading at grade level in the second grade but by third grade Kristina was reading below grade level. Mom continued:

> By third grade I think it was just not listening to instructions, not being able to follow instructions, wanting to play all the time, never wanting to sit down and do any work or anything serious. There were a lot of things I could see that just didn't seem quite right. I would say mostly focusing. At that grade level, you could tell her something and it was like she didn't hear you.

A core evaluation was requested and completed in the third grade and the report identified Kristina as having no special needs. When she was in high school, her mom asked to see her file. In it was a summary handwritten by the three people who did that first assessment. It indicated that Kristina's processing speed was slow. Nothing was done for her during elementary school despite their belief about her processing. In fact, Kristina's difficulty in processing had not even been relayed to the mother.

Mom reported the following:

> By the fifth grade she was really overwhelmed and started to shut down. Fifth grade was when she was really freaking out. She would sit for two or three hours and try to get through homework that should have taken only an hour. She'd just be sitting there and get nothing done. She would read an article and have no idea what she was reading. I would have to constantly interpret for her what she was reading. She would come home with five different homework assignments for one night and not be able to do any of them. She would have to do her math and she couldn't remember what she had

done during the day so she couldn't do the math homework. Fifth grade was just so overwhelming.

Mom looked for answers and found what she thought was a solution in the book *Why Johnny Can't Concentrate: Coping With Attention Deficit Problems* by Robert Moss and Helen Duff Dunlap (1995). She noted: "It was like it was the answer to everything. Not that I was convinced she had ADD because she wasn't hyperactive. There were no other problems other than difficulty in getting homework done, but it just kind of opened up a door."

Mom asked for another core evaluation. Although they found that Kristina did have some attention problems, the evaluation team felt like the problem was with the mother—she was putting too much pressure on Kristina to achieve. So Mom backed off.

In the seventh grade, Mom met with the teachers after two months just to get some feedback on how Kristina was doing. One of the teachers commented, "You know, I really hate to admit this, but she's invisible in my classroom." Mom reacted to that statement by saying, "That tells me a lot because how can you know how she's doing in school, how do you know if she's focusing if you don't even know who she is?" The teacher said, "She sits in the back of the room and she's quiet."

Kristina eventually went to a performing arts high school. She struggled through her freshman year when a diagnosis of ADHD was finally suspected by a guidance counselor. Another evaluation was done; a doctor finally diagnosed her and put her on medication. Kristina was not officially diagnosed until December of tenth grade and by then she was failing practically every class. Mom reported, "She was almost a basket case. She was punching the walls. She was angry."

Kristina said that her frustration was due to, "Not being able to focus on the class, understand the class, do all the work that was required. If someone's giving a lecture in class, it's real hard to pay attention especially if it's a subject matter you could care less about. If the subject isn't interesting to me, it's hard to focus on it." She also felt that "If I'm listening to a lecture, I missed something because I was stuck on something that was said earlier and I'm trying to put it all in perspective for myself. By the time I got it, I'd missed something else." Kristina went on: "My head constantly has thousands and thousands of thoughts in a second. I'm always thinking about everything that's going on in my life."

Kristina finally got the help in high school that she had so desperately needed all along. Throughout elementary school she had been a frustrated child who eventually shut down. The symptoms were there; the pattern was just not identified.

Mom said, "I think my frustration was not getting anybody to recognize that she had a problem because she was so quiet in school and they thought she was doing OK. They couldn't see that at home, how difficult it was for her at night. They weren't even aware that there was a problem."

Kristina's story is just one example of the multiplicity of symptoms and characteristics that can be seen in a child who is challenged with ADHD. Understood and respected, the symptoms don't have to signal failure. As you can see from Kristina's story, however, if the symptoms are ignored, frustration, anger, and failure can easily follow.

Identifying Symptoms

I struggled with how best to help everyone understand the myriad of thoughts and behaviors that define this book's storytellers. Although an isolated event or symptom can help us develop understandings, it is the combination that helps us put the puzzle together. These characteristics describe not simply what they do, but also who they are and how they think, learn, behave, react, communicate, survive.

The focus here is on the symptoms of both *DSM-IV-TR* categories—inattention and hyperactivity/impulsivity—and the storytellers' words reveal how these symptoms impact their ability to function in schools as they are structured now.

Inattention

Attention deficit disorder is exactly what it says it is—a deficit in attention. This deficit can manifest itself in many ways. Figure 4–1 reviews the symptoms of inattention.

You've seen the symptoms. I bet you have even had students who exhibit most or all of them.

♦ The child can't complete homework because the assignment book or textbooks have been forgotten at school. If the books make it home, they often don't make it back. If the homework is done, it remains on the kitchen table.

Symptoms of Inattention

Inattention

(a) often fails to give close attention to details or makes careless mistakes in schoolwork, work, or other activities

(b) often has difficulty sustaining attention in tasks or play activities

(c) often does not seem to listen when spoken to directly

(d) often does not follow through on instructions and fails to finish schoolwork, chores, or duties in the workplace (not due to oppositional behavior or failure to understand instructions)

(e) often has difficulty organizing tasks and activities

(f) often avoids, dislikes, or is reluctant to engage in tasks that require sustained mental effort (such as schoolwork or homework)

(g) often loses things necessary for task or activities (e.g., toys, school assignments, pencils, books, or tools)

(h) is often easily distracted by extraneous stimuli

(i) is often forgetful in daily activities

Figure 4–1 DSM-IV-TR's *Symptoms of Inattention*

♦ The child has a backpack or desk filled with wrinkled pieces of paper, papers stuffed into books, and empty subject folders. Nothing can be found, ever.

♦ The child has difficulty with assignments that have multiple parts and needs to be told four or five times to do something—one step at a time.

♦ The child has difficulty completing tasks, often loving the process, but turning in sloppy and incomplete products.

♦ The child seems to be a poor listener or, on the other hand, seems to be able to respond even when you don't think he or she is listening.

♦ The child can at times listen to and comprehend five conversations at the same time but can't listen and take notes at the same time.

♦ The child seems to have good reading skills, but can't seem to remember what is read.

- The child has difficulty putting thoughts into writing—the mind seems to be moving faster than the hand; handwriting is often sloppy.

- The child is a daydreamer, staring out the window or just appearing to be mentally somewhere else. You seem to have to repeat everything you say.

- The child is inconsistent—sometimes tasks are completed, sometimes they're not.

- The child makes low grades despite what you think is high intelligence.

- The child is frustrated and seems to have a low level of self-esteem.

If you have seen these symptoms, you've probably been frustrated too.

The symptoms are real, just as the people who experience them are real. As students, they are not just trying to get out of doing the work; they are not just unmotivated or lazy. They are, like everyone else, just trying to make sense of the world and to be successful in their small part of it.

Listen to them describe some of their symptoms.

Sustaining Focus

Many of the storytellers described difficulty in sustaining attention or keeping focus. For some it's difficult to focus when someone is talking, particularly if the content is not relevant, meaningful, or interesting.

For others, starting a task, completing a task, or following directions that require sustained attention is difficult. For some it's a deficit in remembering the things you need, in organizing or in losing things. And for some it's focusing on everything at the same time. As Rob said, "It's not an inability to focus. It's the inability to not focus on everything." Sometimes the minds of those challenged with ADHD wander; any distraction pulls them off the task at hand and on to something else.

It is this lack of attention, and the inability to focus for periods of time that make success in goal-oriented schools so difficult. When students can't focus on the lesson, can't remember the assignments, and can't complete tasks, the frustration builds.

Kari

"I kind of lose track of school and think about other things. I think about my dog, my pets, and my family and how lucky they get to be to stay home. Sometimes we have too long periods and everybody gets out of focus and starts talking and stuff. A lot of people are talking around me. It's hard. I get in conversations because I can't concentrate on my work.

"Our arithmetic is pretty hard. It's easier to get drifted off. The teacher sometimes goes off in groups and we can't disturb her. I kind of lose track of where I am, and then I go out into space or something and it's really hard to get back to my work. I just totally drift off and I'm unaware.

"My least favorite subject is probably gym. I just don't like gym because he doesn't do very much exciting stuff, so I definitely drift off. In gym I lose my focus. For half of our gym we do sit-ups or jog in place and do jumping jacks. It's kind of boring. My mind drifts, but my body just keeps moving. When we're doing something really boring or really complicated, I definitely lose track..."

Brandon

"My ADD makes it hard to concentrate when there is really nothing to do. I stare off and think about other things. Concentration is the hardest part about school."

Jillian

"My mother said there was always something different about me. When I was in summer school, I was sitting there spacing out for hours. I wouldn't be paying attention. I was like maybe there is something wrong. I always knew that there was something different about me. I couldn't learn a certain way that most kids could."

Nick

"I always had teachers I could get along with, but it wasn't enough to make me focus. I never had behavioral problems or anything like that in school. It was more just kind of staying focused with what was going on in the class. I was never really a talker. I would doze off and not really be able to pay attention.

"The teacher would say something a little louder and that would catch my attention. I would pay attention for a couple minutes. I would always catch myself drifting off but catching myself didn't do anything. I just realized that I was doing it."

Starting or Completing Tasks

Another symptom, directly related to the loss of focus and attention, is difficulty with getting started on a task; in following directions once the task has begun; and in completing work, be it schoolwork or a task at home. At times just beginning something is the most difficult; it could be that the task is not meaningful or interesting. Or, it could be that too many ideas are rushing through the brain and it's difficult to contain them in order to begin. If a task requires multiple steps, the first step may be forgotten by the time the last direction is given. No wonder so little actually gets completed in the form it's supposed to be done in.

Grant

"I have so much trouble just starting something that I don't want to do. Like if I have a paper for a class that I don't like or care about, I can't even start it really. It's just so difficult for me and even when I do start it, it's so difficult for me to keep with it. My concentration is just not there at all. It's harder for me when it comes to things I don't like."

Nicholas

"I have an inability to buckle down. It's spring break and I've put off five assignments—two or three will be late when I turn them in. I haven't done them. That's pretty much how it's gone. I have trouble getting work done. I wish it were easier. I don't really envy the intelligence of anybody. I envy the work ethic that some of these kids have."

Kari

"If mom tells me to go upstairs to clean up my room, I'd go upstairs and I'd forget what she told me to do. I'll go and stand in front of the mirror and model, or turn on a CD and listen to it and dance or pick up my hamster and stuff. So to help me she just tells me one thing to do and I have to remember it, and then do it. When I'm done she goes up and checks to see if I've done that and then she may give me another project to do."

Kari's Mom

"We have to give her only one direction at a time. We'd have to say, 'Kari, look at me,' because she either wouldn't make eye contact, or if we didn't get her eye contact to look at something, she wouldn't hear us. If she was watching TV, we would have to turn it off, or we would have to go stand between her and the television to get her attention because she just didn't hear us."

Belkies

"No one ever understood that I had a problem. They always thought that I was really smart. My problem was that I wouldn't sit down to finish my work. I didn't think I was smart though. My grades were always really bad, Bs and Cs. The only thing that I was great at was art.

"If something was important or I knew I needed to do good, I would try to study but for some reason I couldn't do it. I always said to myself that there was something wrong with me.

"My parents were always talking down to me and telling me that I was lazy and irresponsible. Right now, thinking about it always makes me want to cry. I always think that the teachers should have known. I had the same behavior at home. I would lose things. I could never finish things."

Alex's Mom

I didn't get a chance to interview Alex but I did interview his mother. Alex, both of his brothers, his mother, and his father all have ADHD. Alex is an example of a child who exhibits little hyperactivity. His symptoms are primarily attentional. Shortly after his sixteenth birthday, Alex dropped out of school. The following is what his mother said about him.

"I do remember that he was very quiet. Those were the kinds of reports that I would get from teachers. He's very, very quiet and he's such a nice boy and things like that.

"It was really in fifth grade that he very quickly fell apart and just couldn't seem to keep track of things. He'd be at the desk in tears. He couldn't remember what he was supposed to do or if he was supposed to do all of this or part of this. He liked his teacher very much but homework was not getting done, class work was not getting done. Then something started really coming to a head. By the time he got to middle school, he fell apart.

"After seventh grade we were really worried about him. One time when I was on his case about homework, he broke down and it took me aback. He just dissolved into tears and screamed at me. He just said, 'You have no idea what I put up with day after day.'"

Jill

"I can't finish a task. I can never ever finish. I'll start gung ho and I can't finish."

Organization

Organization is often a problem for students with ADHD. Look in the backpack or desk of anyone with ADHD and you'll often find a mess. Rob used to say, "I just don't have the half second it takes to put it where it belongs. There are too many other things to do."

Dave

"Chaos is just not having a filing cabinet for a brain. It is hard to sort it out if it is too full and there is too much going on. It is that the runners in my filing cabinet are sticky. My desk is a mess and it always is. I have boxes and boxes of papers that have never been filed. I don't have time because I need to shut the world out."

Grant

"The biggest thing that I've had to work on since I was a kid and was diagnosed is organization. It's just always been hard for me, notetaking, keeping things together in one place for school, keeping things straight and organized. I try to have as little stuff as possible. It helps me to stay more organized to have less stuff. I just throw everything away."

Forgetting and Losing Things

Perhaps most frustrating for many people with ADHD and for teachers and parents is the symptom of forgetting or losing things. Memory problems may result from the inability to attend long enough to process an idea. Whatever the cause, whether in that backpack, in that desk filled with wrinkled pieces of paper, and/or among papers stuffed into books, that homework assignment; that letter for the parent; that permission slip; that pencil, ruler, protractor, compass, or reading book just cannot be found.

Forgetting things—always. Rob said, "The hardest thing about school was remembering to bring a pencil. If I didn't, I would get in trouble."

The child forgets to take books home in order to do homework. If the books are taken home, the assignment book may have been left at school. If everything makes it home and the homework is done, either the homework or the books get left at home the next morning.

The child loses things. It's an interesting phenomenon. The student has something in his or her hand, goes up to give it to the teacher and by the time he or she gets to the teacher's desk, it's no longer there—never to be found again.

I remember once sending Rob to his room to get his socks. He got two socks out of the drawer and headed into the kitchen to put them on. By the time he arrived in the kitchen, he had only one sock. The second one was nowhere to be found and we looked everywhere—except on top of the curtain rod where we found it weeks later. I have this vision of my second grader walking out of his bedroom twirling his arms with the socks in his hand—one flies out and he doesn't even notice.

Jill

"I try to have a place for my keys because I know I'll lose them if I don't put them right there when I come back in. If I don't put them there they'll be gone. I forget where things are. In elementary school I forgot to take books home a lot. I'd be leaving for the day and I'd have homework and I'd forget to take half the books home and I'd have to be driven back to school so many times. In high school, I'd forget so much stuff it got to the point where I had to make a Bring Home list. After every class, I'd write down because if I didn't have that list when I got to my locker, I'd totally forget."

Kari

"If the TV is on, I tell my parents, 'No, I don't have homework.' Then I just forget that I do have it. I just forget. I do my homework but today I stayed in from recess to do my math because I forgot my homework. I did all the pages, but I forgot to bring it in."

Geoff

"In fifth grade, early in the school year, I was forgetting stuff. I wouldn't have my homework but I really wasn't conscious of the fact that I wasn't doing homework. I would go in there and I'd be surprised. I remember setting up completely on my own, a chart, Monday through Friday, and I listed out pants, shirts, shoes, homework. I forget exactly what I had on there, but I listed everything out so that I could go in the morning and make sure that I had the stuff. That was the first sign of me realizing that I did better if I could keep myself organized."

Distractibility

Lack of attention due to distractibility is common. Someone walks by, a noise is heard outside the classroom, a bird chirps in the tree, someone drops a pencil, someone coughs, someone opens a desk to get something—slight movements, slight sounds, or just objects lying around are enough to pull the focus away for many who are challenged with ADHD.

Belkies

"I used to joke about myself and just say I have ADHD. I would read and something would interrupt me and I would have to start all over again. If you are doing something, I look to see what you are doing. I would try so hard not to. I would be talking and looking to see what other people were doing."

Kristina

"I get more distracted by a movement going in front of my eyes than I do a sound. I'll hear something and usually I don't turn my head and look. I'm able to figure out what the sound was and where it came from. If something moves out of my line of vision, I have to look. I can't control it. I have to look."

Jillian

"I need to have an organized environment so oftentimes I would not study in my room because there's a TV, a radio, my bed, my cat sleeping on my book when I'm supposed to be reading it, and the phone's ringing. I realize I work best in a completely quiet environment. I could listen to music but it would only be to block out noise.

"I have to put my headphones on to have a constant noise. Somebody will be talking and I'll get distracted. With my headphones on I can be focused on the music rather than hearing typing, or having a fan going, or having the TV going, or having the phone ring, or hearing someone's cell phone conversation, or having somebody walk in, or somebody knock on the door, or walk by the room. It goes on and on. That's why when I study I have to close the door."

Hyperactivity/Impulsivity

The other significant symptom cluster relates to hyperactivity and impulsivity (see Figure 4–2).

It is much easier to identify students who exhibit symptoms of hyperactivity or impulsivity than it is to identify symptoms of inattention. The student staring out the window may just become, as in Kristina's case, invisible to the teacher. The hyperactive child is "in your face" all the time; you've seen it.

- ◆ The child talks all the time, constantly interrupts, and wants to answer questions before you even finish asking them.

- ◆ The child gets up out of the seat frequently—to sharpen pencils, throw something away, get a drink, go to the bathroom, get a book. On the way to do all those things, the child touches everything.

- ◆ The child fidgets, squirms, slouches, stands, moves some part of the body constantly—just can't sit still.

- ◆ The child makes noise—talking, thumping, drumming fingers, kicking the chair, kicking the desk, tapping a pencil.

Hyperactivity/Impulsivity

Hyperactivity

(a) often fidgets with hands or feet or squirms in seat

(b) often leaves seat in classroom or in other situations in which remaining seated is expected

(c) often runs about or climbs excessively in situations in which it is inappropriate (in adolescents or adults, may be limited to subjective feelings of restlessness)

(d) often has difficulty playing or engaging in leisure activities quietly

(e) is often "on the go" or often acts as if "driven by a motor"

(f) often talks excessively

Impulsivity

(g) often blurts out answers before questions have been completed

(h) often has difficulty waiting turn

(i) often interrupts or intrudes on others (e.g., butts into conversations or games)

Figure 4–2 DSM-IV-TR's symptoms of Hyperactivity and Impulsivity

♦ The child has difficulty waiting in line or just waiting for a turn.

♦ The child seems to always be in trouble—that's whose name is on the board every day.

♦ The child talks before thinking.

♦ The child may have difficulty interacting with classmates.

Rob

"I didn't pay attention, always talking, bouncing around. I didn't know there was a name for it. I just thought that that's the way it was. I didn't know there was any reason for it. I don't remember much in kindergarten and first grade because I wasn't really paying attention.

"I focus on everything; right now my eyes are darting around the room and I see everything. I see it all. I hear it all.

"I know I am impulsive. Every day is one big impulsive decision. I don't find it a problem. I find it a very exciting way to live."

Jillian

"I don't necessarily get hyperactive. It wasn't as much hyperactivity as impulsivity. I can give you at least three examples of my impulsivity as a child. I had a baby blanket and I wanted to cut it up one day so I cut it up. Or my confirmation pictures in my camera; it got caught so I opened up the camera, cut the camera film out, and ruined an entire roll of film. Or the things I would say sometimes. My foot would be in my mouth half the time and I would be like, 'I didn't mean to say that. I'm sorry'—the impulsive remarks, comebacks, and sarcastic comments. It got to a point where I couldn't really control it."

Belkies

"I was always in trouble in kindergarten. In first grade my mom had to come in almost every week because the teachers said that I was always laughing or always talking to someone else while they were talking. When we would need to grab our pencils and go to our seats, it would take me forever. Sometimes I wouldn't even have it. I forgot my notebook. I would walk around the room when I had to sharpen my pencil. I couldn't sit down and I was always talking.

"I was so hyper all the time and sports gave me an escape. I'm the kind of person that even now can play basketball all day. I get tired, but I still have the energy to go on.

"I procrastinate. I think that it has a little to do with it. I can't sit still—can't concentrate. I am an at-the-moment kind of person, an instant gratification kind of person.

"A coworker of mine, we used to sit down and talk and she always had to grab my leg and say, 'Pay attention.' Or my leg was constantly moving and she would say, 'Who the heck is making that noise?' and I would stop right away. When she would talk, my eyes would wander around and I was not paying attention, but I was trying to. She was diagnosed when she was younger, and she told me that I should get tested. I went to see the psychiatrist and he asked me some questions and gave me a questionnaire. He gave me a list of symptoms of people with ADHD and told me to tell him which ones I had. I had them all. I started crying because I just felt so bad. I said, 'So this is what is wrong with me.'

"When I told my parents that the doctor diagnosed me with ADHD, they said that it sounded like I was happy that I had it. I wasn't happy that I had it; I was happy to know that I had it because it explained a lot of things in my life that I had questions about. It felt like a big heavy weight was lifted off my chest.

"My mom blamed me. They always called me irresponsible and said I needed to take life seriously. Even when I told them, they laughed at me. They said, 'We're not laughing at you but it just seems funny,' and I said that it wasn't funny. 'I forget things, but I remembered that you told me that I was irresponsible and lazy.' Sometimes I think that my dad might have it because he forgets a lot, and he has trouble reading because he can't concentrate."

Inconsistencies

Although it is not a characteristic listed in the *DSM-IV-TR*, inconsistency seems to be a common and misunderstood aspect of ADHD. Sometimes a child can focus or attend and sometimes not.

Jill

"It's easier for me to do it sometimes than others. Sometimes I'm just motivated to get things done and I'm like, 'OK, I'm going to do this right now.' Sometimes I can't even fathom doing work. I wouldn't even be able to pull out the book and open the page. Sometimes I can't even sit down at the desk and start to do it. I get these little bouts of attention where I can sit down and do something. I've got to take advantage of this and do my homework right then."

Geoff

"This is the weird thing. It was like sometimes I could read fine and then other times it was like my head was clouded or something and I could not. I would read at a snail's pace and it was horrible. I remember it being hit-or-miss. Sometimes I could just do it and it would be fluid. It wouldn't be a conscious thing. Once I realized, once it became a conscious thing, then there it goes, there goes that state of mind."

Nick

"Some days I would be in class and I would do my work fine and there would be no problem. Then other days I would just be in class, not even thinking about anything, just looking out the window or whatever. Anything else that was going on would catch my attention. I didn't really care about what was going on in class."

Understanding what Jill, Geoff, and Nick say about inconsistency is significant. A common perception by teachers is that if students can do it some of the time, then the times it can't be done must be due to laziness or lack of motivation. If the student would just try, the problem would disappear. I have heard teachers say the following: "If he would just pay attention, we wouldn't be having this problem." Or, "I just don't understand why she does so well in one class but not the other. I think it's just a matter of choice."

I don't know why there are inconsistencies or what to do about it. Many factors play into a child's ability to attend—too much stimuli, too little stimuli, little interest in the task, too much interest in the task making it difficult to break focus. Being aware of the tendency, being flexible, and attempting to understand are part of the solution for inconsistent attention.

Jill's Story

Jill seems to have it all—both the inattention and the hyperactivity/impulsivity. Her story points to the complexity and multiplicity of the symptoms.

"It's like I've got everything going on in my head, all the things I should be thinking about, everything that's going on that day, what I should be doing that day. I don't know if it's just that I'm thinking of all that or I just can't focus on this right now. I start thinking, I know I can't focus, so that means I'm not going to be able to focus, so what's the point of even doing it? The other stuff is swirling around in my head a lot—I'm going to do this later on today, and I'm going to do this, and 'Oh yeah, there's that.' There are just so many different things going on in my head.

"If I go to do homework, I can do it for fifteen minutes. It takes me about fifteen minutes to get into doing the homework. I can sit there and do it for fifteen minutes depending on what it is and then I have to get up and walk around—I'll paint my nails, or go to the bathroom, or take a shower, come back and do some more; get up, go visit some people, come back do some more. The only thing that will keep my attention is if I'm doing something that has a bunch of things involved like going online, then coming back and writing stuff and then putting stuff together in a portfolio. Doing many different tasks at once will keep me focused. Other than that, I can't sit and do it for long.

"With my homework it's worse because I want to be able to get it done but I can't. Like some people sit there in the lounge for three hours straight and do their homework and get it done. In the lounge, forever for me is like twenty minutes. I always thought it was normal because I do my homework by myself so I didn't really think of how someone else did it and how bad it was. My roommate can sit there and bang out a paper in two hours all at once. I just can't comprehend that. I wouldn't be able to. If I sat there at the computer, I'd stare at it for over twenty minutes. I wouldn't be able to do it. Like I just can't. Papers kill me. I can't get a full thought out because every time I start, I get up and walk around. I can't focus on it.

"I just thought my friends were naturally smart—that it came easy to them—and there was me and it didn't really come easy for me.

"I have a real bad fidgety problem. What drives my friends crazy is I'll sit there and my foot will go ten thousand times a minute. They'll notice it, and I can't notice it, and then they'll put their hand on my knee and say stop and I'll say, 'What' and they'll say, 'You're shaking again.' My feet go nonstop. I have to get up and walk around in class all the time.

"My mind just goes all over the place. If I'm talking to you, I'm not really looking at you, I'm looking at all the things in the room. Everything. To remember something I have to write it down about four places and tell five other people. It's not for them to remind me, it's for me to remind myself.

"I always interrupt people. I'd always get in trouble for talking, just talking. I always yell out things. I could never raise my hand and wait on the teacher. I can't wait for someone to finish the sentence. I'm trying to think how I want to answer the question before they finish asking it. They don't know what is going to come out of my mouth next. I am a very verbal person and here it is right now and that is what I am going to tell you. I interrupt people a lot because everything is going so fast in my mind that I don't really think about stuff.

"I get in trouble at night when I go to sleep because that is when I am not doing anything and all I do is think about the things that are going on in my mind. There are so many things going on in my mind that it is ridiculous.

"I can't focus on one thing at the same time. My mom said it was because I was lazy and just didn't want to do it. If I'm reading a book that I like, I could sit and read it for hours, but it's because I'm very interested in it. The whole time I'm reading the book, I would be in another world, focused on it but my hands and feet would be moving. You can't get my attention when I'm reading because I'm so entranced in it. I have difficulty doing that with books for class.

""I talk before I think. It takes so long for me to talk things out. I just can't get it out in any shape or form. It's frustrating. With actions, I'll either not think about it or I'll think about it to death, way more than I should. Should I get up and walk out of this class? Is that rude? Should I do that? Do I really need to go? Am I thinking I need to go but I don't need to go? It's either five minutes of that or I'll just get up and walk out."

Jill commented that she had seen the *DSM-IV* criteria and that she fit all of them. I showed her the list: Fails to pay attention to detail—"That one." Sustaining attention—"Yes definitely." Easily distracted—"Obviously." Is often forgetful—"I forget everything." Hyperactive—"This is my biggest one. I'm always on the go. I talk way more than excessively." Impulsive—"Always. I can't wait my turn. I always interrupt. I have all of these. All of them is me. I have all of them. Especially with the hyperactive and impulsivity."

So What Now?

I asked Jessie during her interview, "Does the world sometimes not make sense to you?" She replied, "Every day. All the time." When it comes right down to it, the teachers' job then becomes helping the students with ADHD make sense of the world.

Understanding and identifying symptoms are only helpful if that understanding translates into strategies for success in the classroom. Once you begin to sense the frustration, you can start working with the student to find out what will help.

As in Kristina's case, the symptoms don't have to signal failure. They can simply be the beginning of a journey of discovery—a journey that will help teachers understand and reach their students.

Creating Safe Learning Spaces

During his interview, Geoff expressed the importance of ensuring that students feel safe while at school.

> I remember hating going to school in the first grade. I couldn't even tell you what we did in that class. I just remember it being pretty traumatic. I remember a feeling of not being safe. There was a coldness about it. Everyone else knew what was going on but I didn't. I didn't have a clue. That's really all I can remember. I just remember feeling like everyone else knew what they were doing and I didn't.
>
> For example, I remember that the red pencil thing was huge. I never had my red pencil. I always lost my red pencil. Everybody else had a red pencil and I kept losing mine. My teacher made the biggest deal out of it. She singled me out in front of the class all the time.
>
> That was when she would interact with me, when I did something wrong. It was bad enough so my parents pulled me out of that school.

Teachers are confronted with a myriad of issues every day: large class size, a lack of supplies, mandates, standards, high-stakes tests, diversity of culture, diversity of learning style, diversity of learning readiness. And into the mix comes the student with Attention Deficit/Hyperactivity Disorder (ADHD).

Students with ADHD are confronted with a myriad of issues every day: difficulty sustaining focus, inability to attend, constantly losing things, impulsive behaviors, organizational difficulties. And into the mix comes the school with a focus on product, a reliance on timelines and deadlines, an emphasis on high-stakes tests, rows of hard desks, walking in straight lines, and the need to be silent when others are talking.

Students with ADHD often hand in messy work, late work, incomplete work with misspelled words and poor handwriting. The problem may be that the student doesn't have the skills to complete a task. If the student does have the skills, he or she may wonder why the task has to be done. Why write down something they already know? The problem may be the inability to focus long enough on the task at hand to complete the assignment. Or, perhaps the student simply forgot what was due or didn't even know it was due because he or she spaced out when the assignment was being given. Whatever the problem stems from, teachers all know the result—incomplete work and another failure.

That lack of success is tragic. The ADHD student is at risk for drug and alcohol use, dropping out of school, and depression. Why? For them, failure is all too common. Here are Rob's thoughts about failure: "If I try something, I might fail. If I fail, I feel bad. So I stopped trying. At school I don't try and so I don't fail. Then I feel good. Until the end, when I fail. Either way I fail and that doesn't seem fair."

So What Can Teachers Do?

What's a teacher to do? This mystery that's called ADHD often defies understanding and explanation. The frustration of the students as they struggle to make meaning of the world mirrors the frustration of the teachers who want so desperately to see them succeed. When confronted with failure day after day, either as students trying to learn or as teachers trying to teach the ADHD student, some may just shut down, give up, and wait it out.

◆ How do you plan instruction for an entire class when you have one, two, three, or more students who space out or disrupt the class?

◆ How do you proceed with instruction when impulsive students waylay everything you plan?

◆ How do you help the child who can't remember that there is something to remember?

◆ How do you get the books home and the homework back?

◆ How do you take all that energy and move it in productive ways?

In an era when no child is supposed to be left behind, students with ADHD often are. The solution is elusive.

The best answer to "What's a teacher to do?" probably lies in creating an alternative school that truly provides an alternative for the unique needs of the students with ADHD, but that's not likely to happen very often. The reality is that these students are in classrooms and are going to stay there along with large class sizes and mandated testing. Teachers can't change the mandates or who is in their classes, so they need to figure out what is to be done.

Caring teachers work very hard to meet student needs. Jennie's teacher called at 7:00 A.M. every morning to make sure everything was packed and ready for school. Most teachers are trying. Most want all students to find success. But many teachers often just don't understand ADHD and don't know what to do. When a teacher does not understand ADHD's nature and makes requests and demands that a child has difficulty understanding or doing because of the nature of the disorder, the student's frustration surfaces. Sometimes a simple request, a regular class routine, or what seems like an obvious expected behavior becomes seemingly beyond the scope of the student.

That red pencil became the focal point throughout Geoff's schooling. School was not a place where he felt safe and could find success. The feelings resurfaced in the fifth grade when he began forgetting things he needed for school. He commented, "It started to remind me of the red pencil"—a time when he wasn't safe in school.

Geoff's mom remembers his first-grade experience clearly although she didn't know about the red pencil. She said:

> By April, he was hysterical Sunday night anticipating school. I'd read him a story and he'd start crying because it was bedtime. He didn't want to leave me. I just couldn't figure out what is going on here. What I concluded about first grade was that if you didn't behave in that class, the teacher lit into you in a very terrifying way. My theory is that Geoff was terrified that she was going to get angry with him when he couldn't get a sound or a letter. He grew increasingly resistant to going to school.

And Geoff was only in the first grade.

Geoff's story of the red pencil is not unlike Jennie's story of the yellow paper, which the teacher required students to use for their math. The teachers demanded something that seemed straightforward and relatively easy—have your red pencil and use yellow paper. Because of the tendency to lose items, forget things, or make a mess, the red pencil and the yellow paper became a metaphor for what school represented. No red pencil, no yellow paper—the result was an unsafe and frustrating school experience.

The storytellers were asked what teachers did or could have done to help them become successful. They talked about adaptations and instructional methods, about curriculum and homework modifications. Most often, however, they talked about the interactions they had with their teachers. Listening and understanding became the key to helping them achieve success. The relationship with the teachers or principals was one of the key factors in the success or failure of the students.

The first place to start may simply be a change in attitude and a change in the way teachers relate—a bit of flexibility and bending. The students interviewed wanted to be liked, to be respected, to be treated like human beings. That shouldn't come as any surprise. When teachers believe in kids, support them and lift them up, they are more successful. When teachers demean them, put them down, fail to validate, and/or accuse them of being lazy, they fail. Dave sums it up: "If you constantly get shut up, you are going to start giving up."

What Dave is talking about, unfortunately, happens more often than anyone would like to admit. Teachers may not understand ADHD or they just may be frustrated after having tried everything and finally give up. Whatever the cause, whether it be the red pencil, the yellow paper, or some other incident, all the storytellers could remember sometime when they were demeaned, put down, or not validated.

Kristina talked about the time she got sent to the office for what she says was, "asking my friend for a highlighter." She described her visit:

> I got in a big fight with the vice principal because he looked at my grades and saw how bad I was doing. He called me an idiot in front of the teacher who sent me to the office. He told me, "How are you going to survive in high school if you're going to be like this." I said, "I'm going to the performing arts high school" and he said, "You're not going to get in that school. You're not smart enough. They only take smart people there." I broke down crying. I couldn't believe someone had said that to me.

So what can teachers do?

A Little Change in Attitude

I want teachers who really love Kari. Even though Kari could be very frustrating, they could appreciate who she is. —KARI'S MOM

I like it when a teacher treats me like a person and not just a student. Like if I'm acting up in class, Mrs. S. doesn't just say, "Rob, shut up." She says, "Rob, when you're talking in class, it's distracting me so I can't explain what I'm trying to explain." Don't judge the kid as a problem child until you get to know the kid. Most teachers if they see you talking the first day, you're a troublemaker. —ROB.

Time and again the storytellers said that what they wanted was to be seen as human beings with thoughts, feelings, ideas. They wanted to be treasured for the gifts they brought to the classroom, not demeaned for not being able to do it the way everyone else does. They wanted to be listened to, not just the words that were said but also the words that weren't said.

Schools need educators who don't just see these students as dysfunctional, disobedient, disorganized, disabled, or disturbed. Educators should be able to flip all those negatives around and see the positives. As Rob said, "I'm not disorganized. I'm widely distributed."

Schools need educators who can see the spark, talent, intelligence, and enthusiasm of these kids. Teachers need to see the potential and harness that energy and excitement along with the disorganization to ensure success at school and in life for students challenged with ADHD. It may mean changing a routine, changing the curriculum, or changing instruction. It certainly means changing attitudes.

The ADHD students who succeed have teachers who believe in them. Those teachers recognize that there is a neurological dysfunction called ADHD, and that despite it, they are dedicated to helping students find success. Weiss and Hechtman, authors of *Hyperactive Children Grown Up* (1993), followed children with ADHD for many years into adulthood. Dr. Weiss concluded: "When the adults who had been hyperactive were asked what had helped them most to overcome their childhood difficulties, their most common reply was that someone (usually a parent or teacher) had believed in them" (cited in Zeigler Dendy 1995, p. 22).

Be Nice

Most teachers work hard to develop lessons that are active and inclusive. They agonize over appropriate instruction for ADHD students and should. But what Kari, Geoff, and Nick wanted most was for teachers to be nice. "This is for all teachers, to be nice to the children and if they don't understand something, don't just say, 'That's wrong' and get all mad and stuff. Try and be real nice and helpful," Kari said. Here are Geoff's thoughts.

> What mattered most to me is if the teachers were nice to me, someone who doesn't get aggravated. Someone who can keep their cool, a teacher that won't show that she had other obligations and maybe would take a little bit of time to help me with something, wouldn't show frustration, wouldn't get worked up, and would be easygoing. Most importantly, to like what they're doing.

Nick agreed.

> Certain teachers helped me out in the class, put in a little extra time, just to be nice. That would be the only kind of thing that would help me get into a class and pass it. It's such a huge difference on how you have to deal with somebody. It's best if the teacher doesn't get frustrated with having to help even every day. Kids with ADHD need to be dealt with [by] a teacher who can kind of roll with the punches. They're more often not real hyper and they need someone who can kind of understand that.

With all the worry about how to differentiate instruction, teach organizational skills, or design a curriculum, it's comforting to know that one of the most important keys to success with students with ADHD is to be nice. For Kari, Geoff, and Nick that meant teachers who were willing to go out of their way to be helpful, who didn't get upset if the students didn't understand something, but thought it was their responsibility to figure out a way to help them understand. These teachers didn't blame the students for not grasping a concept, and the teachers didn't give up but just kept at it.

Kristina had both types of teachers—the teacher who was willing and had the skills to help her find the success she needed and the teacher who wasn't willing or able to help her. She knew that she worked harder for those teachers who gave her extra help. "It does depend on the teacher. If the teacher is not big on helping me, I won't approach them but if I know it's a teacher that's understanding or I know will help me, I will approach them." Kristina continued: "[I] met with this one teacher and said, 'These are the kinds of problems I have with things.' When the time came when [I] had to write a report, I would say, 'This is really difficult reading for me. I need help.' He wouldn't give me help."

She became perceptive over the years: "If I notice that a teacher isn't going to be a very supportive person and isn't going to say, 'Yeah I understand what you're going through and I'll let you do the assignment this way,' then I'm just like, 'Yeah, whatever. I don't want to deal with you because you're not going to help me.'"

Show Respect

Rob loved his sixth-grade teacher. Her curriculum consisted of authentic student choice lessons that often involved drama and other active hands-on projects. That alone would have been a good enough reason for loving her. It was the first time his energy was seen as an asset and his creativity was allowed to flourish. When asked, however, why he liked her so much, Rob immediately commented, "She treated all the kids as if they were really smart and she had faith in their potential."

Peggy Sullivan, an eighth-grade social studies teacher, told me about a student on her team. This student misbehaved in all the classrooms except hers where he was almost a model student. The other members of the team wanted to know Peggy's secret. "How can you get him to behave? What is your management technique?" She told the other team members the secret; it was simple: "He knows I think he's wonderful."

Listen

One of the key pieces to being treated with respect is being listened to. When someone feels they are listened to, they gain power over their thoughts and feelings. They begin to realize that what they think and say makes a difference. Rob said this about the teachers at the performing arts high school where he transferred his sophomore year:

> The teachers there understood my issues more so than others, much more. A lot of power was transferred over to the students. The teachers were friends and not just teachers. A teacher was a person I could learn from, I was a person that a teacher could learn from, and there was that general understanding between all the teachers. They listened to me. I want teachers to listen to me more instead of just standing up there teaching and going through the motions—to actually listen to what the kids are doing. I'm not even just talking about listening to words—I'm talking about knowing what's going on in life.

Rob wanted teachers to listen to not only what he said but also to what he didn't say. He wanted teachers who knew that he was more than just those things he missed on tests.

When students feel that teachers or administrators are not listening to them, they lose their sense of power, their sense that what they say makes a difference. For Nick, this feeling that he didn't matter led to his leaving school.

> I had a lot of bad experiences with our principal in situations where he never seemed to be paying attention or willing to listen. That made me stop going to school about halfway through the year. We had a big meeting with all my teachers, two of the principals, both my parents, and my tutor. After that meeting, I felt really bad. It was a real depressing scene, just trying to get a word in. Everything I said there was a "Yeah but." Every point I tried to make in terms of saying, "I have ADD. I'm not looking for a gift or anything, I know I shouldn't get any real breaks but I do have ADD." Whenever I would try to explain something, the principal would say, "Yeah, yeah." It got way too depressing for me so I just walked out of school. I never went back to sign out.
>
> They would say they were listening and you could tell they were just kind of saying it to get you moving along and get in what they had to say like, "Oh, I understand that but..." I was just frustrated because it wasn't that they couldn't understand because I knew that they could. It's just that they were choosing not to. It's like they already had their minds made up before the meeting. A lot of the teachers were pointing out good points too which was nice, but they would have to say what the problem was in class and they would offer a way to get around it and say they were willing to work with me.
>
> But the principals, they get the bad things on one sheet and they have the whole picture on another sheet. The bad sheet is what they refer to. They don't really take the time to look into things. It never seemed like they wanted to do it. There was never anything positive that came out of them.

Getting to Know Students

In order to affirm students, teachers must truly get to know them and become "kid-watchers." From the first day of school, a teacher should be dedicated to knowing each and every child. For elementary teachers with twenty to thirty in a classroom, the task of knowing students is relatively easy. The team approach helps middle school teachers because they can collaborate with teammates about specific students. High school teachers have a more difficult task. With sometimes more than 150 students a semester, it's harder to get to know each and every one.

Teachers have developed many ways to record their observations of students. Some have a clipboard with a card for every student taped on it. Throughout the day, they write down any observations about each child's interests, strengths, difficulties, frustrations, and successes. Other teachers have labels on which they keep information. When a label is filled, it is stuck in the master three-ring binder that contains a section for every student.

What goes on those labels or cards? Everything. A child comments about a little league game, a student shares a concern about a cat, someone struggles with a math concept, someone else can never seem to find the right page, one child is always humming or tapping her foot, another has difficulty with multipart instructions. The key to these lists of observations is the analysis of the information. It's looking at each page for each child and finding patterns in behavior.

One child may be a mystery, so the teacher might focus on that child for two or three days, trying to figure out an entry point. When did that child get completely engaged in the work? What did I do? What was the topic?

The technique of recording information about every child works best for elementary teachers. But, how can middle and high school teachers connect with their students? With ADHD students, the hyperactive ones are easy to identify and remember. Some students are in your face and you'll remember them immediately. It's the silent students, those staring out the window, who become almost invisible. Look for silent ones who seem to fade into the classroom environment without you ever knowing they're there. If, after a couple of weeks of school, you don't know a student's name, or anything about him or her, make an effort to talk to that student—even five seconds may do the trick.

If teachers are dedicated to knowing students, they stay open to relationships with them. It is important to get to know each and every child. Listen to them—not just to their words but also to what goes unsaid. Listen to their behaviors. Get to know students completely: their interests, their learning styles, their readiness levels, their difficulties, their point of motivation, their lives. During this process, teachers will begin to fall in love with each and every one of them. Students cannot and must not escape our hearts.

How can you give up on a child whom you know so completely and whom you have grown to love? Every interaction with that child is then based on what you know to be true about him or her. Through continued observations, you can refine and expand that truth. You are listening to and respecting the truth of that child's life.

Does knowing so much mean that suddenly the child will become easy? Not necessarily. What it does mean is that you now have the most powerful tools to help that child find success. You have information about the student as a learner and as a person. And you have a relationship based on respect. When that child leaves you after a year, maybe he or she will not have made straight As or developed all the skills or understandings you were hoping for; however, that child will feel successful, which can empower him or her to keep at it. For one year at least somebody believed in that child—someone like Rob's sixth-grade teacher who treated him as if he were really smart and who had faith in his potential; someone like that eighth-grade teacher whose student knew that at least one teacher thought he was wonderful.

Advice in a Nutshell

Relationships are important. What can you do to develop them and support students? From what the storytellers said, and from what a number of teachers have passed on about what worked in their classrooms, the following list contains some advice about how to establish a caring environment for learning. Most of these points are obvious. It's up to every teacher to critically reflect on their teaching and to try to incorporate most or all of these ideas into daily practice.

♦ Remember, ADHD is a neurological condition; it is not the child's fault. He or she should not be punished for not being able to do something.

♦ Listen to what the student has to say—both spoken and unspoken. The student knows what he or she needs.

♦ Respect what the student is telling you.

♦ Use the student's name, all the time.

♦ Care about and support a student's interests inside and out of school.

♦ Respect the life that this student is living every day—trying to make sense of the world.

◆ Take the time to do small things that can help: Supervise packing of the backpack, checking to see whether all needed materials are there.

◆ Make sure assignments are written down clearly.

◆ Check in with the student a few times a day.

◆ Never give up. Never ever give up.

◆ Keep your sense of humor.

◆ Don't sweat the small stuff—set the priorities right. Forgetting a pencil is small stuff. Opening up the possibilities of the world through learning is large stuff. Do anything you can to make learning happen.

◆ Be nice. Welcome the child. Tell the child you are happy he or she is at school.

◆ Allow for movement and for a quiet space in which to calm down.

◆ Keep a can of red pencils or a pile of yellow paper on your desk.

◆ Be patient.

◆ Remind rather than ridicule.

◆ Value each and every student; value the individual gifts and talents each brings to the classroom and to you.

◆ Be flexible—everyone doesn't have to be doing everything the same way at the same time.

◆ Ensure success every day in every way.

◆ Be helpful not harmful.

◆ Remember that no one is perfect.

Advice From the Storytellers

Educators know that when a student feels safe emotionally, he or she will be more likely to succeed academically. If a student does not feel valued, that student sees no reason to try to do the work. The storytellers gave advice on how to create a positive environment for learning—how to create safe learning spaces.

Kristina

"Be patient. Take the time to sit down and read the student's IEP and talk to the student and see where [he or she] is coming from. Get to know the student. See the person as an individual because not everyone with ADD has the same issues and problems, I'm sure."

Kristina's Mom

"I think these kids don't have a lot of trust in adults and I think that's the first thing—to gain their trust."

Jillian

"Don't get down on them and don't ever call them stupid. Always be open-minded."

Rob

"My advice to teachers is to relax. Just basically relax and realize that not everything that happens in school is a big deal. A perfect teacher would be energetic and really get into what they're teaching and actually know about what they're teaching."

Kari's Mom

"Be patient, and be flexible and not judgmental about these kids. Talk to their parents. Try to learn a little bit more about what these kids are like outside of school and appreciate them. I want people to appreciate Kari's personality."

When dealing with everything that happens in classrooms today, it's almost refreshing to hear that the most important thing teachers can do for students with ADHD is to be nice, to listen, and to build relationships. Everyone is capable of that. Although some may not know how to adapt a lesson, provide the exact academic support or best graphic organizer, deal with late and forgotten assignments, get students to listen and stay seated, get them to focus, help them be organized, all teachers can let a child with ADHD know that he is smart and that she is valued—that together they'll work to make every day a successful one.

With changed attitudes, teachers can appreciate the positive contributions that students with ADHD bring to the classroom and can learn to value their energy, enthusiasm, and different ways of looking at the world. In other words, stop trying to force them to do just what you want and begin to design a learning environment that truly meets their individual needs.

Jennie's Advice to Teachers
Every Student Is Different

I don't think there's anything specific you can do because every kid is different. Look at them as individuals. Don't expect every ADD child to be the same. You have to find out what works for them. Help them try different things. Come up with a plan that's appropriate for them. If it works for one, it doesn't need to work for everybody. I think that teachers really need to learn to be flexible. I think each individual teacher has to make his or her classroom the best it can be for what the child needs.

What about color-coding things—social studies, red; math, purple? Color coding worked for me and if it's going to work, that's great. If it doesn't work, we'll try something else. I think also a homework folder that everybody has is always helpful. It's easier for the kids to stay focused. One homework folder to go home with you. It doesn't leave your bag.

If it doesn't work, I think teachers just need to be flexible about it. What about this? What about that? Let's try things. What do you think will help you?

Learn about your kids, know about them. The more you know about them, the easier it's going to be. Pull them aside, ask them, "What about your day is the most hectic?" If you know that at noon the kid is off the wall, you're not going to be doing a math activity and sitting down, doing nothing. Know when the child is capable of doing quiet work and when the child is not. The more you know about them, the more you can help them structure their own day.

Some teachers want to force the child to be normal. They want to find the route that makes them like everybody else. They want the child to become what they need them to be instead of the reverse. A lot of teachers feel like kids need to change so they fit in instead of realizing that the teacher needs to change to make the kid fit in. They figure if the kid could just be normal then we won't have a problem. "If I could just find a way for them to pay attention, everything would be fine." I think if you structure your classroom around what your kids need and when they do their best, even your kids who don't have attention deficits, or aren't labeled that, they're going to succeed more—they're not being forced to sit down and do something quiet when they really want to move.

I think with kids, you need to let them find their way. They'll come up with their own strategies. As a whole class, talk about how they work, talk about study strategies, social skills, everything. I think when you grow older you almost develop them yourself but I think supporting them is the key.

If you give them the strategies by engaging them now as children in the second, third, and fourth grade, when they get into the fifth grade, they're going to be able to spend a little bit more time on more structured stuff. Say it's a complicated problem; if they can't do the whole problem at once, do the steps together, engage them, and then little by little you pull back. "I'll help you with the first half of the problem, you do the second half." By the time they get to sixth, seventh, and eighth grade, I think it's going to be a little bit easier. But you still give them help. In high school be supportive; you still treat them as individuals.

If it's really complicated, what's wrong with acting out, what's wrong with getting manipulatives? Or what's wrong with taking it piece by piece? What are the different steps you can do? "Do a step and we'll talk about it and then do another step." It's wrong to just say, "Here's the problem. Here's a piece of paper, now do it. You have four minutes."

Manipulative: getting the class involved and going over the steps. Talking about how many steps there are. Not expecting that they will just sit down and do it because they're not able to. Most kids are not going to be able to do a complicated problem. Maybe some kids, but not all kids and especially not kids with ADD.

Classroom setup is important—keep the students facing the teacher. I used to hate when the teacher's back was to me. I used to wander off. I always sit in the front of the classroom because it's easier for me to focus. When I sat in the back of the row, I would pay attention to everybody. Everybody caught my attention, and I could never focus on the teacher because there was so much in between me and the teacher. I can't handle all the stimulation in between. If the kid works better sitting in the back seat, great.

Give them stuff that's interesting to them. Engage the students. Keep things active. Don't bore them to tears. If the kid likes computers, let them go on the computer, let them research, let them have fun. I think it's important to move in the classroom, that you allow them to walk or have stations around the room where you can get up and get stuff. Even if it's something simple like paper, it exerts enough energy to let you sit through the next five minutes. I think it's OK to have noise. I hate rows too. Kids need to be in a horseshoe or clusters or something.

Let them sit near their friends. A lot of people say you can't stick ADD kids near friends or they won't pay attention. I think that sometimes they almost pay attention more because if their friends are closer, they're not staring across the room at them. If their friends are closer, they're going to feel a little more confident. If it creates a problem, obviously you need to move them, but what's wrong with trying?

I think you should be [upfront] with your kids, "This is what I'm expecting." Have the kids set the classroom rules. I think if you just pay attention to what each kid needs and tell them what you expect from them, you'll have so much less hair ripped out of your head. And don't ridicule kids when they scream out—it's not their fault.

Give them the opportunity to grow and succeed. If they succeed in things, they'll have confidence, and if they have confidence, they're going to do better.

What to Teach and How to Teach It

A Look at Curriculum and Instruction

We don't want less work. We want different work.

—ROB

The success or failure of any child, particularly one challenged with ADHD is founded in relationships. When teachers have those positive relationships, they can enter into negotiations that provide students with voice and choice. Although a repertoire of good teaching strategies will help, what is most needed is a determination to talk with students, listen to them, and elicit their help. Once those relationships have been developed, the next step is to create relevant curriculum, develop best practices in teaching, provide adaptations when needed, and help students become organized so that they can complete their work resulting in a high-quality product.

Attention Deficit/Hyperactivity Disorder (ADHD) is a medical diagnosis, not an educational one. Yet teachers see the results of ADHD in the way that it impacts students' ability to learn and function in classrooms. Difficulty in sustaining attention and getting work done, forgetting and losing items, acting impulsively, and having difficulty sitting still are going to have an impact on a child's ability to have success in school. Work comes in late, incomplete, or too sloppy to read; behavior is inappropriate. The student may be able to read but can't sustain interest or focus long enough to comprehend what is being read. In elementary school, recess is missed because of one infraction or another. In middle or high school, suspension is a frequent punishment. It's only in looking back that the storytellers can begin to identify how their learning was impacted by ADHD.

This book is not about best instructional practices. Such books have been written and can provide you with numerous examples and suggestions about teaching methods to help students reach their maximum potential (see Bizar and Daniels 2005; Daniels, Hyde, and

Zemelman 2005). This book is about reflecting on your practice to see how you can help your students with ADHD be more successful academically by making some changes in what you're doing. It's about listening to ADHD-affected students and, from their stories, learning about ways you can interact and adapt to breed success.

How ADHD Impacts Learning

Listen to what the storytellers have to say about how ADHD affected their ability to be successful in school.

Grant

Grant was diagnosed in the seventh grade but had struggled in school from the beginning. He had difficulty completing assignments and became very discouraged. He had the most difficulty with reading. Although Grant didn't have trouble with the structure of reading, it was sustaining focus long enough to comprehend what he had read that caused the problems.

"In elementary school I think my first signs were around third or fourth grade. I always had trouble completing tests and assignments, especially math. I didn't like to read. I'm a very slow reader. In high school and middle school, I really hated to read because it took me a long time and I would have to read things over and over again. I would find myself at the end of the chapter and not remember anything that I had just read. I wouldn't be paying attention to what I was reading and realized that I would have to go back and reread it all over again. When I was concentrating on something, I could comprehend it very well. It was just a matter of focus. It got to the point in middle school where I was just sick of school already and I hated going.

"In the seventh grade my mother was concerned because I wasn't doing well in school. It was not the hatred for school because I kind of kept that to myself; more not doing well. She had been reading stuff about ADD. I remember she got a book about it and read several of the passages to me and I was like, 'That's me. They're describing me.' So she found a doctor who specialized in that area.

I was relieved at first to have a label put on it, kind of as an explanation for why all this stuff happened to me. But there was also a part of me that made me feel like there was something wrong—to have this disorder that you can label yourself with. It kind of made me feel like I was different from the other kids and there was something wrong with me."

Nick

For Nick, the requirements of school got more and more difficult as he got older. As schooling got more difficult, it also became more meaningless to him until he finally left.

"Through fourth grade everything was fine. About fifth grade, I failed my first class. Then sixth grade I failed a couple of classes. Junior and senior year I felt like I wasn't getting anything. Anything I learned I wouldn't retain it. It just wouldn't seem valuable to me.

"I could read and I could comprehend as I was reading but when I looked back at a chapter, things would just kind of get all scrambled and stuff.

"About two-thirds of the way through my senior year, I just couldn't bring myself to go. I tried. I talked to my parents and I kind of felt bad about leaving. I didn't want to disappoint them so I would get up in the morning and I would go. I would just sit in the parking lot for five minutes and it would be just enough. I would just be like, 'I can't even be here' and I would turn around and leave. That was the one place I had ever been in that could possibly depress me. I had never been in a situation that seemed that depressing."

Belkies

Belkies' ADHD made it difficult for her to complete tasks. She ended up failing classes because she just couldn't finish the required work.

"In elementary school, I had trouble learning how to read. I wanted to read because I loved to learn things but I had trouble sitting there finishing books that I was reading. I liked what I was reading but I couldn't focus on it. I failed a couple of classes. I think that I failed because I couldn't sit down to do the math thing. It was the one thing that I hated the most.

"In college I feel that at the end of the semester I really have to push myself to go to class. It's like having to fight with two people in my head—one telling me to do the right thing and the other saying, 'Nah, just relax.' It is a good attitude and a bad attitude because it doesn't make me think of the consequences when I do things.

"I do want to finish school, it's not like I don't. I actually like school. I love the learning."

Jillian

Jillian identified her mind as the problem. She would lose attention or focus intently on something that she wasn't supposed to be focusing on. Like Belkies, she also had a struggle with the two voices in her head telling her to do competing things.

"I must have spaced out during most of it [school] because I don't know it now. It's like, was I ever taught this? I was always doing something. I'd pay attention in class, but then sometimes I would just stare at somebody. I'd listen to what they're saying and I could be having a whole different conversation in my head with myself. I would ask a question and people would say, 'Where did you get that from?' and I'd have to go through the process. It's amazing. I used to be able to sit for hours on end and just think.

"If I knew that I had to pay attention to something, I could get my mind to do it except my mind's completely strong-willed and says, 'You don't want to do this.' It talks back to me. A lot of time I have to justify myself and sometimes I don't feel good enough.

"The world can be hard sometimes when you don't know how to say something. You have it on the tip of your tongue but you can't say it and you think of it but it comes out all wrong and the person you try to tell it to gets offended."

ADHD with its related symptoms has an overwhelming impact on the way students learn and behave in school. Before teachers can identify ways to modify the learning environment, they need to look at the nature of curriculum and instruction.

A Look at Curriculum

When a curriculum is designed, paths for student success or student failure are created. A look at curriculum and the way to design it then become important steps in finding ways to meet the needs of students with ADHD. Because they are easily distracted, these students need to find meaning in what they are learning and to know how they can apply that information in their lives. All students want to find practical meaning in curriculum; for the ADHD student, however, it is critical. If we don't grab them with meaning, they'll be lost.

Altering curriculum is difficult. With district, state, and national mandates and standards, teachers have specific content they need to teach. Students have a right to learn that content. The task then becomes to help students access content in ways that are relevant to their lives. This did not happen when Rob was in school, as he noted.

> The most upsetting thing for me is that all the stuff they taught me to focus on in school hasn't come into play at all now, like remembering a pencil or putting my name on the paper. I don't see writing a research paper coming up in my lifetime. Those skills were not as important to me as say learning to speak to a crowd. It was just useless stuff that made my life miserable for twelve years.

Using Essential Questions and Broad Understandings to Ground Curriculum

One way to help students see relevance in what they learn is to center units and teaching around broad understandings and essential questions that transcend specific topics and tie learning together. When identifying the standards teachers want to meet and framing them into a unit of study, they first need to look at why it is important for students to know this information—to identify the broad understandings students should develop. What will it teach them about themselves and the world around them?

A study of the Civil War teaches students about conflict, oppression, discrimination, and how one person can make a difference. As a result of such a unit, students should understand that conflict occurs when people disagree about the best way to do something. They should understand that sometimes conflicts end violently although it is possible to work toward nonviolent solutions to conflict. Students should understand that oppression occurs when one person or a group of people feels that they are better than another group. They should understand that the actions of one person can change the course of history. Those are just some of the broad understandings that might arise out of a unit about the Civil War. Notice that these understandings don't specifically mention the Civil War; they focus on the central reasons why that or any war is studied.

Out of broad understandings, teachers develop essential questions that drive the unit. Wiggins and McTigh (2005) in their work, *Understanding by Design*, discuss the use of essential questions:

> These are questions that are not answerable with finality in a brief sentence—and that's the point. Their aim is to stimulate thought, to provoke inquiry, and to spark more questions—including thoughtful student questions—not just pat answers. They are broad, full of transfer possibilities. The exploration of such questions enables us to *uncover* the real riches of a topic otherwise obscured by glib pronouncements in texts or routine teacher-talk. We need to go beyond questions answerable by unit facts to questions that burst through the boundaries of the topic. Deep and transferable understandings depend upon framing work around such questions. (p. 106)

The essential questions that might drive a unit on the Civil War could be: What causes conflict? How does the oppression of a group of people guide their behavior? What do people do when they are oppressed? (See Figure 7–1 for examples of essential questions for several subject areas.)

A question such as "What causes conflict?" relates to life. That's a different question than "What caused the Civil War?" That doesn't mean students don't need to find the answer to the causes of the Civil War. That information is just tied into something broader. Students can then find answers to questions about other battles and struggles, including those in their personal lives. Post essential questions and keep going back to them. "What have we learned about the causes of conflict? Have any of you experienced a similar situation?"

But what about those standards? Next to the essential questions on the wall, post the standards. Let students know that this list is what they need and have a right to know about magnets, electricity, rocks, colonial America, the civil rights movement, measurement, writing good essays, and so on. Continue to refer back to both the questions and the standards throughout the unit.

Authentic Learning Experiences

Centering the unit around essential questions and broad understandings creates opportunities for powerful learning experiences. Giving students a voice in planning those experiences is a way to begin. When

Representative Essential Questions

Social Studies
◆ How do things change over time?

◆ What causes conflict?

◆ How does the past influence the present?

◆ What impact does the physical environment have on life?

◆ How are cultures similar and different?

Science
◆ How does the physical world work?

◆ How are living things similar and different?

◆ How are we all connected?

◆ What's out there beyond us?

◆ How does the makeup of something impact its function?

Language Arts
◆ What makes a good book?

◆ What makes a good reader?

◆ What does a book tell us about ourselves?

◆ How do writers communicate what they want to say?

◆ How does writing change depending on audience?

◆ What does a book tell us about life?

Math
◆ How do numbers help us understand our world?

◆ What do good problem solvers do?

◆ What do patterns reveal to us?

◆ When is it better to use estimation rather than exact numbers?

◆ What does "finding the unknown" have to do with success on the job?

The Arts
◆ What makes something beautiful?

◆ What does it mean to create something?

◆ Why do people create?

◆ Who determines what art means?

◆ How does art change people's feelings?

Figure 7–1 Representative Essential Questions

students are given choice and voice in negotiating the curriculum, they are more willing to invest time and heart because they understand why they need to complete a learning task. In other words, the learning is meaningful to their lives. You can start by having students generate questions and concerns about their own lives, the world around them, and the topic being studied.

The next step is to work with students to design experiences during which they can find answers to their questions while they actively manipulate the information through hands-on activities and are given opportunities to process and think about new understandings. In an attempt to gain understanding and answer the essential questions, and the questions they have about themselves and the world around them, students explore, investigate, research, communicate, create, and think deeply about issues. They become historians, scientists, mathematicians, and writers who use learning experiences to help make sense of the world.

Authentic experiences allow students to use the skills that they are learning in ways that people in the real world would use them. Scientists don't read chapters and answer the questions at the end. Scientists make hypotheses, set up experiments, gather and analyze data, form conclusions, and then start all over again. Scientists also read to gather the data they need to solve problems.

Mathematicians use math to solve problems that require mathematical thinking. There are no real math problems in the world— there are only those problems that need math in order to solve them. Historians read and analyze primary source documents and draw conclusions by looking at multiple points of view.

Good citizens (the goal of a social studies program) help make decisions, communicate, compromise, and solve problems. People use reading, writing, and speech to communicate thoughts and ideas. While students may need some direct instruction to learn specific skills, using those skills in an authentic context is what makes the learning meaningful.

Let's look at a unit on rocks. The essential questions might be: "How does the physical world impact life?" or "How do things change over time?" Students need to understand that the makeup of the world has a great impact on how society has developed. Knowing the best way to build shelter, plant gardens, or use rocks in various creative ways can make people's lives easier. Students should also understand that the Earth is constantly changing.

Teachers can teach students those concepts by creating learning experiences that will allow them to think deeply about the essential questions. Students can use the lens of a city planner, a geologist, a gardener, a builder, or a child going camping. In order to do any of those things successfully, content becomes important because it helps them to explore specific questions: "How can the materials around us be used to best plan our city?" or "What do we need to know about the physical world in order to plant a garden?"

Throughout the unit, students will be examining rocks, discovering ways to test their hardness, learning how those rocks were formed over time, and classifying rocks. In the end, they will be able to answer specific questions about planning a city or surviving in nature. They also will be able to answer the essential question: "How does the physical environment impact life?"

Nothing was more authentic than Grant's senior year in high school when he took a trip around the United States with a teacher and nine other students.

"It was amazing. The funny thing is, out of the ten kids that went, most of us were the bad kids. We were the kids who were in trouble, that were tired of being in high school. We didn't really want to be in high school anymore. It saved a lot of us. It was perfect for a bunch of us.

"We would go out on a trip for anywhere from two weeks to five weeks, and there would be a theme for each individual trip. It was seven or eight individual trips. We did one that was a U.S. history trip. We started in North Carolina and drove up the East Coast. We went to Gettysburg and Antietam and then we came to Boston.

"We went to Canada and stayed with one of the girls—her aunt and uncle knew some guy in the Parliament in Canada and we talked to him. We had the Native American theme—we stayed at a reservation at the bottom of the Grand Canyon. We drove in a bus everywhere—he would teach us some math on the trips and we did a lot of science too.

"When we went out West, we did geology. We would be rafting down the river through the canyon and he would explain what the formations were. I never ever before cared at all about geology, but when I was there and seeing these rock formations, it was interesting and I learned it and remembered it. I would never remember anything like that if I had just read it out of the textbook in a class.

"I learned more in that year in school because I was out seeing stuff. It's always been hard for me to sit in classes and learn about something just by thinking about it. It was so much more exciting to go out and see things that we were learning about. Read about something and go do it and see that this is what we're talking about. It's not just some passage in a textbook."

Teachers usually can't take students on trips like Grant's, but they can find ways to make classroom learning authentic. Designing authentic experiences requires that teachers look at instructional strategies. If you want to bring the Grand Canyon into the room, do it through the instructional choices that you make.

A Look at Instruction: Teaching to Diverse Learners

Howard Gardner reminds us that not all children learn in the same way. His theory of multiple intelligences (Gardner 1983) opened educators' eyes and their understanding to the idea that there are many kinds of intelligence. While some students will thrive in discussions, others want to see, feel, or act something out; as Belkies noted, "I think you have to grab their attention with something they like. Find different ways to teach the same thing and find what they like." Some students want to draw murals or illustrate their stories. Others learn by rhythm and beat. In the second grade, Rob said, "If teachers would only sing everything, I could get it."

It's not possible to take every lesson that's taught and meet every intelligence or learning style every time. Teachers can, however, provide opportunities for students to learn in their strengths as much as feasible, while providing opportunities for them to strengthen their weaknesses. They can also provide alternative forms of assessment so that students can demonstrate what they know.

In her work on differentiated instruction, Carol Ann Tomlinson (2001) continues to advocate for designing instruction that meets the needs of all students. Her work focuses on creating learning experiences based on educators' knowledge of students' readiness levels, interests, learning profiles, and affect. While all students are expected to master the same broad concepts and to meet the standards, they may be doing so while reading books at different levels, completing problems at different levels of abstract complexity, or presenting information through different modes.

Teaching to multiple intelligences and differentiating instruction are not easy, but when teachers know their students well and are willing to elicit their help, authentic learning experiences for all students become a reality; and teaching, as a result, becomes exhilarating.

Grant went to the Grand Canyon. While there, he learned something about geology, history, and math. What made that experience so powerful for him was that he actually got to touch and feel and see what he was learning. He asked questions and then found the answers to them. It was authentic learning at the highest level. He became a geologist, an historian, and a writer.

All students can't go to the Grand Canyon but teachers can bring the Grand Canyon to them. They can't visit a rain forest, and for most students, a trip to Boston is out of the question. Students can't do a deep sea dive to study underwater life or climb into a volcano to learn about rock formations; however, teachers can bring visuals in for them to see. They can bring in artifacts for students to touch and CDs with sounds for them to hear.

Learning experiences centered around questions to be answered can be created—questions posed by students or by the teacher in consultation with them; for example: How did the formation of the Grand Canyon impact the culture of the people near by? What is freedom? How did the actions of individuals help the formation of our democracy? How are all living things interdependent? Why was Washington, DC, designed the way it was? How does a city's design affect the development of civic life in that city?

Authentic learning means providing students with the opportunity to use their minds in real ways to solve real-world problems. It allows students to use skills they have learned to make decisions. Teachers can teach students how to analyze primary sources in history class, then they need to allow them to do so. Teachers can teach them to design experiments, then they need to allow them to do so. Teachers can teach them the parts of a letter, then they need to allow them to write real letters to real people.

I asked the storytellers what helped them learn. What you will discover is that what they are talking about is just good teaching. There is nothing magical about what they said. They were the most engaged in lessons that were active, hands-on, and gave them some choices and control over their learning. They talked about making learning relevant, meaningful, and fun. They talked about having direct connections with those things they were learning. They talked about constructing their own understandings about knowledge and about truly understanding something, not just spitting back facts. They talked about what they will truly value and use in their lives. In addition, they saw a great need for flexibility on the part of the teacher.

Nick

"I always did better with hands-on. In class when we had projects, made something, or worked in a group—some type of hands-on activity, that was always good. In terms of reading from a book, listening to somebody else read, I could never stand that."

Jillian

"Hands-on things are always good. I would learn through relating to something. I learned by having a catchphrase and having fun activities in school. I remember the teachers who did the fun things were the ones I learned from, not the teachers who would sit there and lecture, give us reports, and not have fun. Always be open-minded. You have to deal with a lot of problems you don't get paid for, but it has its benefits because you see the little kids with a smile on their faces. If you see that kids aren't catching on, try a different approach."

Kristina

"It makes a big difference if the teacher's up there lecturing and doesn't like it if you interrupt and ask questions. If they're like, 'No wait until I'm done,' I'll forget by then. This teacher would write things on the board, too, and would go really fast. He'd write his own notes on the board and we'd all copy his notes and later on I'd look at the notes and think that the notes made no sense to me. He'd move so fast it was hard for me to write my own.

"My Greek and Roman Civilization teacher tells history like a story. He'll give a Spartan general a voice and tell it like a story and act it out and draw diagrams of battles on the board like he was planning for a football game. We just sit anywhere in the classroom and be relaxed. If you have questions right away, you can ask him. He'll gladly answer you. It's obvious that he is passionate about the subject. He's a very funny guy and he'll make you enjoy the class and he'll grab your attention. It hasn't just been him teaching the class. It's been us too. You're more likely to pay attention to a peer. He brings history to life."

Rob

"My best teacher was Brian. He never used a chair. He always squatted on the ground or was running around the room. He always used his hands. He pointed and he always got into what he was teaching about. He loved it and got really passionate about it."

Jill

"There are certain teachers that I do better than others because of the way they run their classes—like it was a getting up and doing activities class. I could do good in the class. If they kept me on track I did good. If they gave me homework if it was something I'm interested in, I could sit there and do it very well. But if it's something I'm not interested in, I'm horrible. I can't focus my attention."

Brandon

"Try explaining things more thoroughly and try to do a little more hands-on work instead of just making them take notes and do mind-numbing work. Let them be themselves, think by themselves."

Belkies

"I think you have to grab their attention with something they like. I liked sports so that was really interesting. I liked art. Find different ways to teach the same thing and find what they like."

Jessie

"It's important that I understand what they're talking about. I want teachers who are excited about the subject matter. It's important that the teachers are excited about it, they understand it, and they have creative ways to present it."

Kari

"I think you should be able to get up and walk around, just to walk around to ask the teacher something. And you don't want to let the kids not be able to eat the whole school day. And they should always have a break so you could read to the children or something like that."

Advice in a Nutshell

Authentic teaching is not just having fun activities for students to do. That may make school fun, but it doesn't necessarily make it meaningful. Meaningful activities come out of the broad understandings you want students to develop. Teachers often find a unit topic, then say, "Oh, here's a fun activity to do with that unit." For example: It might be fun during a unit on the Western states to make cookie-dough maps of the states. You can use pieces of candy to indicate mountains, rivers, major cities, and so on. When done, everyone can eat it. That sounds like fun. Does making cookie-dough maps meet your goals? Does it answer essential questions for the unit? Does it lead to broad understandings? Will it lead students into the unit? Will it motivate them to want to learn more?

Look at the standards, identify why that topic is important and relevant for students, identify essential questions and broad understandings, and then collaborate with students to design powerful learning experiences. When teachers do that, they reach more students and have a curriculum and instructional design that is particularly suited for students challenged with ADHD.

Curriculum and Instruction that Works

♦ Give students choice and voice

♦ Identify broad understandings and essential questions

♦ Explain the importance of the material

♦ Choose high-interest tasks

♦ Teach to multiple intelligences

♦ Build movement into lessons

♦ Use graphic organizers

♦ Provide hands-on experiences with time to process

♦ Have fun, but do it within the context of authentic learning

♦ Give frequent feedback

♦ Use games to enhance motivation

♦ Present each concept through various activities

♦ Use multiple modes of learning (see it, say it, write it)

♦ Break activities into smaller pieces

♦ Do small group lessons and find a group that each student can function in

♦ Be passionate about the subject

♦ Give yourself permission to modify

Tying Symptoms to Learning
What Teachers Can Do

How do we make chickens feel better? How do we
prevent them from pecking each other to death?
Let the chickens go free.

—DAVE

Quality relationships, relevant curriculum, and authentic instruction are the first steps in helping students with ADHD be successful. Sometimes, however, they are not enough and teachers have to make modifications and adaptations in the physical environment or in the way students have the opportunity to access information, process learning, or demonstrate their understanding.

The key to success for both the teacher and the student is to take the understandings about the way students with ADHD function and turn these understandings into successful strategies for learning. Teachers' task is to develop modifications that can help these students begin to make sense of their world so that they can be successful in school and in life.

Right to a Good Education

Students with ADHD have a right to learn the skills and concepts that are being presented in school. They have a moral right to learn, and they also have a legal right. Two federal laws were passed to help students with ADHD: IDEA (Individuals with Disabilities Education Act of 1990) and Section 504 of the Rehabilitation Act of 1973. IDEA guarantees all students a "free appropriate public education." Although ADHD was not recognized as a specific "handicapping condition" under IDEA, a 1991 memo from the U.S. Department of Education (USDE) indicated that students with ADHD could be covered under the section of IDEA that includes "other health impaired." (In the memo, the term *ADD* is used to recognize both *ADHD* and *ADD*.) The USDE memo states that "children with ADD should be classified as eligible for services under the 'other health impaired' category in instances where the ADD is a chronic or acute health problem that results in limited alertness, which adversely affects educational performance" (Davila, MacDonald, and Williams 1991, p. 3).

If a student is not eligible for services under IDEA, he or she may be eligible under Section 504 of the Rehabilitation Act. This act is a civil rights law that prohibits any agency receiving federal funding to discriminate based on a disability. Under Section 504, a disability is anything that limits one or more "life activities," including learning. A "504 Plan" can be developed to stipulate how the student will have access to learning and what modifications will help that child be successful.

The 1991 memo, in addition to describing rights under IDEA, describes the responsibilities under Section 504. The memo states that teachers should be trained and aware of the manifestations of ADD in the classroom and provide adaptations that include:

> providing a structured learning environment; repeating and simplifying instructions about in-class and homework assignments; supplementing verbal instructions with visual instructions; using behavioral management techniques; adjusting class schedules; modifying test delivery; using tape recorders, computer aided instruction, and other audiovisual equipment; selecting modified textbooks or workbooks; and tailoring homework assignments (Davila, MacDonald, and Williams 1991, p. 7).

Other modifications that were described in the memo include "reducing class size; use of one-on-one tutorials, classroom aides, and note takers; involvement of a 'services coordinator' to oversee implementation of special programs and services; and possible modifications of nonacademic times such as lunchroom, recess, and physical education" (Davila, MacDonald, and Williams 1991, p. 7).

Students with ADHD whose ability to function in the classroom is impaired have a right to either IEPs or Plan 504; that is the legal imperative. Whether or not a student has been evaluated by the school district and deemed eligible for such a plan, teachers can and should modify their instruction for him or her. That is the moral imperative. All students have the right to find meaning in school and to experience success.

Being aware of a student's strengths can help teachers find the entry point for helping them learn. For elementary teachers who have the same students all day long, watching them react to different modes of teaching can facilitate discovery of what works best. Middle school teachers who work on a team can collaborate with teammates in identifying strategies. It is more difficult, however, for high school teachers who may interact with as many as 150 students a day. If you teach in a regular education classroom, not everyone will need modifications. You won't have to be designing twenty-five individual lesson plans. Focus on the few students who have ADHD. Talk to them, ask them what works best, and help them identify strategies that work.

Students want to be listened to and can become their own best advocates, but they have to be taught how to do so. Students need help identifying how they best learn. Flexibility and constant communication become the keys to success. As Jennie says in her advice to teachers, "Learn about your kids, know about them. The more you know about them, the easier it's going to be." She reminds us to work with students from the beginning to teach them strategies, help them identify those that work, and give them a voice about their own learning. Students need to learn to advocate for themselves—to be able to say to a teacher, "This is what works for me."

Kristina noted that she didn't learn to advocate for herself until she was in high school; "I approached my Greek and Roman Civilization teacher and I said, 'All right, this is who I am, these kinds of things are difficult for me. Sometimes this works for me, sometimes this works for me.' I told him things like that and he sat there and he said, 'All right, we'll take it as it goes.'"

Conventional Logic

By looking at the symptoms of this neurological disorder, it is easy to see why learning or behavior problems occur. The student's attention and behavior problems are not due to laziness or lack of willingness. The student is not being stubborn or just refusing to listen. The student has a neurological disorder. Teachers need to accept that and get on with addressing the learning process.

Conventional wisdom tells us that if a child has a weakness, teachers must remediate for that weakness by giving him or her more of what the student is bad at. If a student has a reading comprehension problem, whether due to an inability to attend or to an inability to process, conventional logic tells us to increase reading instruction—

one-on-one or in a resource room. Now the child has reading, language arts, and an extra hour of reading. For half the school day, the student has to read, something he or she doesn't like and doesn't do very well.

For students with ADHD, this approach often has the opposite effect, reinforcing a sense of failure and negative attitudes toward school. It would be better to look at what the ADHD student is successful at and give more of that. If a child is a gifted athlete, increase his P.E. time. If a child is getting As in science and doing poorly in other classes, do more science. If the child has a great understanding of technology, let her help in the computer lab. Teachers must become advocates for students and write the necessary structures for each to succeed into their IEP or 504 Plan. Put aside conventional logic and reinforce students' strengths rather than focusing on the weaknesses.

Strategies

Any strategy that you use can be effective—not necessarily for everyone and not necessarily always. ADHD students are all different and what one student responds to may not be what the next one responds to. Something that works one day may not work the next. Effective teaching is not about having a "bag of tricks" to motivate the child with ADHD. It's about listening, respecting, and responding. Teachers need to continually dialog with students about what's working. Do something and tell the student to try it for a week and to let you know how it's working.

Helping Students Complete Tasks

Students with ADHD often have a difficult time with multistep directions. The first step is forgotten by the time the third step is given. It is difficult for them to focus long enough to keep all the steps in mind.

If you say, "Please get your math books out, turn to page 196, do the odd numbered problems, and when you're done put the paper in the bin and begin reading," most likely you will hear the following: "What was it you wanted us to do?" On the other hand, you will have students in your class who can do all those things immediately and are eager to get on with it. They don't want to have to wait between each instruction.

You don't need to make modifications for everyone in the class but for those students with ADHD, giving the instructions one step at a time will help them get started on tasks. Give the instructions to the whole class, then go back and repeat them one at a time. Other options include having them written on the board or on a handout. Proximity and eye contact also help.

Students with ADHD also often have trouble completing assignments with many steps. Breaking an assignment down into simple steps and allowing students to work one step at a time is helpful. That doesn't mean less work; it means doing it in stages. Maybe the student does three problems, shows you what he or she has done, and then goes back to complete three more. For a major project, you can assign small pieces of it rather than give the whole thing at once. Work with the student to find the best balance. Ask them, "What would work best for you to finish this assignment?"

In addition to breaking down instructions and assignments, it's important to break the school day into manageable pieces. One high school had a twenty-minute rule—every twenty minutes, the teachers would change activities. In elementary or middle school you might have a fifteen-minute rule. Start with a discussion, switch to direct instruction, then to a demonstration and a hands-on activity. End with a time to process and reflect. Jill described one of her teacher's procedure:

> He'll do the notes then, "Does everybody understand it?" and then he'll do an activity for that specific little chunk of notes. Then we'll start a new one. Before we're done with it, he'll go over it with examples. The next day he'll go over the stuff we did the day before to make sure we understand it. It's like reinforcing it so many times that I have to pay attention, which is good for me.

Alternative Assignments

Some teachers feel that the solution to incomplete assignments is to give less work to the student with ADHD. When everyone else has to do questions 1 to 10, they only have to do the odd numbers. Although less of a workload may be necessary and beneficial in some cases, think of the message that sends to students. In fact, if doing problems 1 to 10 is vital in order for students to learn the information, then all students should do them. If it's not vital, then why do any of the students have to do them all?

If the knowledge is important, your job is to see that students have ways to learn it, understand it, and to let you know they understand it. Teachers don't want to give students with ADHD the message that the information and work is important for everyone else to know but it's not important for them.

Making modifications doesn't mean giving less work or lowering expectations. It may mean giving different work. The way you think about your instruction and assignments will translate into more appropriate teaching for all students and the ADHD student will reap the benefits. Can they write stories, dictate answers, create a radio broadcast, write a play, compose a song, choreograph a dance, conduct a survey, graph some data, make a poster, make a model, give a speech, tell you what they know orally, write a myth, design some costumes, develop a lesson for a younger grade, have an informal chat? Can the material be keyboarded and immediately emailed? Yes, and all without sacrificing standards and expectations.

Rob said the following about two assignments he had in science class. Given his handwriting difficulties, he asked the teacher whether he could approach the assignments in a different way and she agreed.

> In science the assignment was to write a story about a certain type of rock. I was thinking that it would be more fun to make a webpage about a rock. So I got on the Internet and got all the information about rubies and people named Ruby and businesses with Ruby in their name and put it on the page. So not only did I learn about rubies, but I got to do something I enjoyed.
>
> For another assignment we were supposed to make a 3-D model of an atom. So I got on my computer again and made a 3-D movie of protons and all the electrons spinning around. My sister, who works at a news station, made it possible for me to stand in front of a blue screen like a weather forecaster and point at the atom and explain it. I handed the video in. I got an A on both assignments.

Both of the projects indicated that he knew the concepts and the content. The teacher rewarded Rob for the work in demonstrating his knowledge. For a time the teacher questioned what she would do if she had no tangible product to read or put on the shelf with the other students' work. But she was willing to rethink how she would assess her assignments, and Rob was the winner.

What If It's So Sloppy You Can't Read It?

Another problem for many students with ADHD is handwriting. Whether this sloppiness is due to a handwriting disability, lack of attention, the brain working faster than the hand, impulsivity, or processing difficulties, often the child with ADHD produces sloppy, illegible work. You can't read the answers on the test. Essays are short with incomplete sentences. Spelling is horrible. The chapter outlines are incomplete. Notes taken in class are illegible. Worksheets are half done and sloppy. Whatever the cause, sloppy work is common. As Rob says, "If I worked five hours on a project or five minutes on a project, it would look the same. Why should I work harder when I know the quality won't be any better?"

For some students, the solution may be to alter the assignment so that handwriting isn't required. Can they dictate answers, make a video, create a webpage, keyboard the work?

If you want students to take notes during class, try giving them an outline of your lecture notes or a template to take notes on, with the major headings already listed. You can also give students copies of your notes to review for the test. You can assign a note-taker—someone willing to use carbon paper when taking notes or whose notes you can make a copy of for the student with ADHD.

It goes back to the task. Are you requiring students to take notes so that they will learn to take notes? In that case, a template will help the student organize the note-taking. Are you assigning note taking so that students can study for the test? In that case, a scribe or copies of your notes are needed. If it's important enough to study and learn, the child should have an opportunity to do so without being penalized for poor handwriting or processing.

One student's Algebra teacher gave him copies of all her notes and it made a big difference in his grade. He was able to go back and review formulas that he never would have been able to do by looking at his own notes; he can't read his own handwriting. It allowed this student to be successful in algebra class.

Be Flexible

Students with ADHD have difficulty completing work; when you look at the symptoms, that makes sense. Lack of completion may be due to an inability to sustain attention to the task, not following through, the inability to organize, losing things necessary for the activities, being distracted, or simply being forgetful.

One beneficial modification is time flexibility. Yes, you want to help students become responsible. While helping them learn the strategies to do so, teachers can be flexible about work—both the timeline for the work and the work required. Remember, the goal is learning. If the student learns and processes in a different way and in a different time frame, that child is still learning.

Jillian tells us about a teacher who was flexible with timelines. What is interesting about her comment is that because that teacher was flexible and understanding, Jillian was willing to do a lot of work for her.

> My most understanding teacher in high school had this way of teaching and this way of understanding. One day I hadn't read the entire chapter but we were having a test. I was really stressed out and she let me take it two weeks later when I had read everything. She was one of the most understanding teachers. She always helped me and I always did a lot of work.

Some of the storytellers commented that there were times when they had actually done their homework but had left it at home on the kitchen table. The traditional response would be to give the student a zero for not having homework, make the child stay in for recess, or have the child come in after school to redo what he or she had already done. Flexibility means just bending enough so the child feels success instead of another failure.

Kristina talked about how her teacher was willing to give her alternative projects and oral assessments to document her learning—another way of being flexible.

> I had a lot of teachers who were willing to support me and help me through. For example, if we had a paper to write or a reading packet to do, he usually wouldn't hold me to it. Like with the reading packets, once a week or once every two weeks we would sit down and he would ask me questions and I would tell him everything I knew about whatever he'd ask me. For one class we knew I would have to read this book, so during the semester they bought me the book so I would start it and kind of get myself into it. For the last project, for the last book we read, the teacher said I could do a poster. It didn't have to be some written report. I made a huge poster and I actually did write something but it was an explanation of what all the pictures were. The teacher loved it.

Nick also commented on how time flexibility helped him. "I had extended time if I was late on a homework assignment and that definitely helped a few times."

What About Organization Skills?

I get frustrated that even when I try to get organized I can't so I just stop trying to get organized. It takes too much time to get stuff into my notebooks. I have to move on to the next thing. There's so much stuff going on. Someone's tapping the desk. Someone is whispering. I can't take the thirty seconds to get the thing in the notebook because I might miss something so I just stick it in my bag. —ROB

Organization at any level is difficult for the child with ADHD and yet it is an important element in helping develop successful strategies for work. Although it is difficult to teach organization for what is a physical problem, you can teach ways to cope.

Dave's problem with organization was that his brain was full of too much stuff going on. He didn't have time to organize a paper because he was spending his time trying to shut out the world; this is similar to Rob's problem with organizing. With too many other things to do, he felt he just didn't have the thirty seconds necessary to put things away. Grant dealt with his organizational problems by just throwing everything away. The less stuff he had, the easier it was to get organized.

Organization is a huge issue, and for many ADHD students, it's the key to failure. The homework assignment doesn't get home. If it does, the books to do the assignment have been left at school. If the books get home and the assignments get done, they often don't get back to school. And if they get back to school, the student can't find the assignment in the backpack. If the assignment is found, it's sloppy, wrinkled, and doesn't have a name on it. And when there's work to be done in class, the books are still at home.

A simple technique that helps is to give the child two sets of textbooks—one set stays at home and one stays in the classroom. That way, the student never has to remember to take the book home or bring it back. Your school district doesn't have enough books? Encourage parents to have it written into the 504 Plan or IEP and the district will have to provide two.

In elementary and middle school, particularly, teachers try to teach organization skills using various techniques. One popular technique is subject folders—a different one for each subject. Jennie liked to color code them; that's a strategy that worked for her. Each subject was kept in a different colored folder. When she got papers for a subject, they went in that folder.

For Rob, the separate folders strategy didn't work. Five folders were too many to keep track of; instead, he had one folder. Homework due went in the folder. When it was done, it went back in the folder. Although some teachers tried to get him to save important papers for a test, it worked best when teachers had a folder on their desks in which important papers needed for the future were placed. Did it take a little bit of time on the teacher's part? Sure. Did the teacher have to do it for every student? Absolutely not. But for Rob it made all the difference in the world.

Lack of organization may result in forgetting to bring things needed to complete tasks in class. A teacher can say, "You forgot your protractor. I guess that means you'll not pass the test." Or a teacher can say, "You forgot your protractor. Here's one you can use for the test. What can I do to help you remember next time to bring things to class that you'll need?"

The Assignment Book

Another popular approach for keeping homework assignments organized is to have an assignment book where all the homework assignments are noted. While the assignment book idea is good in theory, three (or more) problems can arise: (1) remembering to write down the assignment, (2) being able to read the handwriting once it is written down, and (3) finding the assignment book when it's time to do homework. Even having parents sign the book causes its own set of problems if any of these problems are occurring.

For Geoff the problem was even more severe. He wasn't paying attention when the homework was given, so he didn't even know it was due. "I wasn't conscious of the fact that I wasn't doing homework. I would go in there and I'd be surprised." He was aware that everyone else seemed to know homework was due. Where had he been?

There are many ways to help students know what assignments are due: email a list to all students, have another student write the assignments down, type assignments and give the child a list, check the assignment book to see whether it's legible, and be flexible if the homework doesn't arrive back at school.

Self-Talk

One of the more powerful techniques to help students become organized and get some control in their sometimes seemingly chaotic life is to teach self-talk skills. Rob had a fourth grade teacher who used to take ten points off every assignment if a name wasn't on the paper, if the date wasn't on the paper, if the subject name wasn't on the paper and if the student's mailbox number wasn't on the paper. Requirements like these meant that Rob got a D on every paper before it was even handed in.

To use the self-talk method, the teacher could tape a card to Rob's desk that lists those four items. When Rob came to hand a paper in, the teacher could say, "Rob, go look at the card and make sure you have done all four things." Notice the teacher wasn't saying, "Have you remembered your name, and so on." Rob is still responsible for the tasks.

The next week the teacher can say, "Rob, think about the card. What are the four things on the card? Have you done them?" Rob is learning a bit more responsibility. Finally, the teacher can say, "Rob, have you done what you need to do before you turn your paper in?"

Maybe the teacher will always have to remind him of the card. But Rob is ultimately responsible for remembering what is there. The card might even be replaced with one that has two check marks on it that remind him to double-check that he has done what needs to be done.

Slowly, through training Rob to talk to himself about the four things, he learns to be responsible for them. The teacher's only task is to remind him of the card. Unfortunately, Rob's teacher refused to try that technique and he eventually had to be pulled from fourth grade because of severe depression due to chronic school failure.

Teach your students to talk to themselves: "What do you need to do before you go home?" "What is the routine before you leave for school in the morning?" This technique may carry students through to adulthood; they learn to walk in the house and say in their minds, "I am going to put my keys here."

Rewards and Punishments

Some people advocate setting up a reward system to help students with ADHD complete tasks—"If you pay attention, I'll give you a free homework pass." Although a reward system might be worth trying, be aware that it rarely works. It's almost like telling someone you will give them a million dollars if they hit a home run in Fenway Park. A reward system was set up for Rob. He was told that by completing all his homework for a week he would earn a computer game. On Wednesday he said, "It's just not worth it. It's too hard."

Equally problematic is the threat of punishment. Taking away recess, giving detentions, or refusing to allow students to participate in extracurricular activities will not take away that person's neurological deficit. Often what is being taken away from the student is the thing that is the most motivating. One student loved baseball and music. The teacher suggested that the student not be allowed to play baseball or go to guitar lessons until he had finished his homework. Why take away the two things that the child was most successful at in order to have him do something at which he was chronically failing? The baseball and music wouldn't become motivators; instead, the work would become torture.

Kristina's mom talked about Kristina losing recess. "Her fifth-grade teacher said if she's not going to do her homework at night, she can stay in at recess. To the kid, who all she ever wants to do is play, that was no motivation to get her work done."

Kristina talked about having privileges taken away if she didn't do something. That didn't work for her. "If I can't watch TV for a week, I'll listen to music and draw. I could always entertain myself. I'd sit in the grass and make pictures. It didn't matter."

Rewards and punishments rarely work. Relationships do.

Modifying the Classroom Environment

It didn't seem like the teachers in the class were the problem and it wasn't the students. It was just kind of the whole surrounding environment. —NICK

Teachers can do a lot with the classroom environment—both the physical and emotional environment. The key is to find the classroom setup that helps a particular student.

Some students want to sit in the front of the classroom so as not to be distracted by everyone else. Some students like sitting in the back where they can see everything and get up and walk without distracting other students. Some may need a cushion to sit on, some a bungee cord around the chair legs so the feet can stay busy. Some may need to hold a rock or other object to keep hands busy. Some might want a desk blocked off from all stimulation. Others might need to see things in order to function.

Kari's mom describes what one teacher did for her.

Kari had a separate little desk in the room that she could go to if she needed to get her work done. The teacher had actually done it in a real positive way. It wasn't a punitive place. It was a place that Kari could take herself to and that helped. Sitting at a table with four other kids, she couldn't do any work. She also let her go and use another table in the room. So Kari would physically take herself and go sit at this table, sometimes with her back to the rest of the class to try and tune that out.

Kari describes the same teacher: "Our teacher is really nice because she lets us get up and walk. She doesn't ever just let us sit and listen to what she's saying. I think you should be able to get up and walk around to ask the teacher something."

How does a teacher find the right amount of stimulation? Dave says that "if the kid is sitting in a room by a window and things are going on outside, I can see how shutting the window could help. I see if you give that kid a wobbly chair or a ball to sit on to get it out of his system—that's just what I think would be good." But an environment without any stimulation could be equally disruptive. This is what Kari said about her ideal physical environment.

> I work best when I'm alone with the teacher in the room where there's no noise and there's nothing to distract me, no open windows and stuff like that. I wouldn't want a desk that's surrounded so you couldn't see anybody. Not just big empty walls. I couldn't do my work. It would be really easy to daydream because there was nothing to do in the room. My mind would break the walls I bet. My mind would kind of just go out of the walls. If I had just a window, it might be a little distracting to look at the clouds.

Allowing students to get up and move as needed as long as they aren't disrupting the rest of the class also seems beneficial. In fact, just knowing there is a way to "escape" is important. That modification was written into Nick's ed plan.

> I was made aware of the fact that I was allowed to get up and leave class whenever if I just didn't feel right. That was on my plan and I just didn't know it. I really wasn't that kind of kid that would go to class and then leave. If I didn't want to be in class, I just wouldn't go in the first place. If I was in class already, if I wanted to leave, I would just sleep.

Middle and high school students with ADHD have an additional problem—a locker full of books. Brandon's mom had quite a few things to say about that.

The kids have so many books to carry to so many different classes. With ADHD they don't have time to think about, "I need this book for this class and this book for this class and then I can come back to my locker later." Brandon carries every book with him. He carries his backpack around with him all day long because he does not have time to do that and because he forgets his books. One time last year he forgot an English book in his locker and the teacher gave him a detention. "Can I go get my book? It's right down the hall." "You're staying after school." This is stuff that shouldn't be happening. You know it's been like this throughout Brandon's entire school life. It's just one big fight after another.

Assessment

They shouldn't grade me on what I can write down on paper. They should grade me on what I know. —ROB

One of the purposes of assessment is to find out what kids know. ADHD students often have difficulty focusing on a written assessment. One student's high school biology teacher was concerned about his test scores. They didn't seem to reflect what she thought he knew based on classroom discussions. His essays were sketchy, his short answers were way too short, the handwriting was illegible, and his spelling was atrocious.

The SPED coordinator suggested an oral exam. After sitting with the student and listening to him talk about genetics, the teacher was convinced that he knew more than anyone in the class. She would never have known that if she hadn't given him an alternative form of assessment.

Performance-based assessments, oral assessments, projects, posters—anything to allow students to let you know what they know. Self-assessment can also be a powerful tool for any student because he or she can analyze their own strengths and weaknesses.

But what about those high-stakes standardized achievement tests? Ultimately, all students have to pass them to graduate. Jennie made the following comments:

I think that if you engage them, critically thinking, doing activities, discovering on their own, then they'll do fine on the test. Definitely kids need modifications if they have other disabilities. They should get them and you should fight for them. I think you should also keep an engaging atmosphere in your classroom. I think that the kids will do fine on the test just because they're going to have to use critical thinking. They may not be doing the textbook and the question things, but I think that kids learn better and will like learning better, almost do better on the test because of less test anxiety. They feel more comfortable in your classroom. It would also be a good suggestion if you could give them untimed tests. That way they can move and you can move them.

With any assessment teachers have to remember that the goal is learning. One of the goals of assessment is to see that learning has occurred. One of my students—a future teacher—was frustrated during her student teaching experience by a fifth-grader who just wouldn't complete his multiplication facts worksheet. When I asked her what the goal of the worksheet was, she said it was to find out whether he knew his math facts. I suggested she ask him. The student teacher came to class the following week and reported that she sat with the student and asked him the math facts and the fifth grader knew them all. Does that mean he never has to write anything again? Not at all. It does mean that teachers should look at their goals and act accordingly.

Assessment Suggestions

♦ Point out impulsive errors made by students on tests and let them correct those errors.

♦ Help students sort out their thinking.

♦ If you know students know the material, allow test retakes.

♦ Test them orally.

♦ Give alternative tests (not your traditional essay or another teacher-generated test).

♦ Let some students have a scribe.

Is it fair for the student with ADHD to have alternatives to traditional assessments? Absolutely. In fact, any other policy would be unfair. Would you test a farsighted student without his glasses? Would you deny a student her hearing aid during a test if she needed it?

How About Pullout Programs?

For some students with ADHD, a resource room with a tutor is written into an educational plan. Both Nick and Geoff benefited from being with tutors. Nick made these comments:

> It was three-quarters of the way through freshman year when I got diagnosed and I got put on a 504 Plan with a tutor. I went to her for one period every day and did studies. I got all the attention I needed. She was really patient and she went out of her way to help me. She sometimes sees something that I didn't even see. She was really good at communicating. I don't know what her tricks were, but she always seemed to get the point across. If I didn't have any work to do, we just kind of hung out and it gave me a break for the day. Sophomore year went really good. I was into soccer and baseball and that kind of kept me in line and helped me focus on getting things done because I wanted to play.

Geoff started in a resource room in second grade. He said he went "to a separate room with a couple of other kids to do flash cards and stuff like that for awhile." Although Geoff felt that the pullout program is what got him through school, he is not sure that it's the best solution.

> I didn't mind it at all because the teacher was nice and that's what mattered most to me. I just remember it being kind of difficult, very difficult, it was just memorization—putting a card up and, "What is this word, what is that word, what is this word?" But with the teacher being as nice as she was, she wasn't coming down on me if I didn't remember. I just remember that being really tough, taking everything I've got and feeling that I'm going nowhere with it. Through high school I had resource room study hall where they had two teachers in there with eight kids and they helped you out with your homework.
>
> I question now the special attention or individual attention. I kind of think back to my childhood when I was receiving that special attention. Doing it because I had to do it. It kind of was this singling out, kind of not aware that there is anything wrong as a kid but a feeling of maybe I just wasn't able to understand that there was something wrong. I felt that I didn't understand like I understand now that there was something wrong. I felt like, "Why is this person paying so much attention to me?"

I know it had to help me but I don't know if that's the best way to deal with attention deficit. I know that that's the reason that I was eventually able to make it through all the grades I did but I kind of feel like it was, maybe it's more complex than I think.

When I was doing it, I think it made my anxiety level rise or low-ered my self-esteem as far as education, like having to get the special help. It's like playing a sport and you get ten extra hours of training than the rest of the team because you're struggling. It's not fun, and it's not anything you want to have to do so in that way it's bad. But it helped me. I think maybe there are better methods but I don't know, other than that I just remember it being stressful. It was toler-able because the teachers I had were so nice and caring and wanted to help so it wasn't traumatic.

I just remember feeling pressured especially doing flash cards because it's like the time of truth. You either know it or you don't. It wasn't being pulled out of class that was bad. It was the complete focus on me and making me work. It was difficult so it was stressful.

A Quick List of Suggestions

The following is a list of suggestions for you to try in the classroom. When you look at it, try to pick those modifications that will help stu-dents cope with the symptoms of ADHD that are giving them the most difficulty. Is the student's main problem lack of focus? Is it con-stant movement? Is it an inability to complete work?

The list is long. That's because there are a lot of options. Communication with students is important as you struggle to find something that works. (Thanks to numerous teachers and students for helping with this list.)

Homework

◆ Have two sets of books for each ADHD child

◆ Check with students on the way out of class to make sure they have what they need

◆ Encourage students to dictate work to parents at home

◆ Write down homework assignments

◆ Remind them to turn in homework

♦ Be tolerant of late homework—be extremely tolerant of late homework

♦ Encourage students to finish work no matter how late it is

♦ Be happy when they turn in homework

♦ Provide alternatives to writing assignments

♦ Give written homework instructions and make sure all assignments are written down

♦ Don't give homework

Class Work

♦ Simplify everything as much as possible (e.g., rules, directions, schedules, routines, choices)

♦ Allow the use of voice-activated software on the computer to dictate answers to work

♦ Maintain eye contact

♦ Repeat

♦ Give students a copy of your notes

♦ Let students use a computer instead of writing by hand

♦ Arrange for study buddies

♦ Try to avoid timed tests

♦ Recognize the special gifts that students challenged with ADHD have

♦ Keep students out of the spotlight by isolating conversations

♦ Lots of one-to-one—make time for them

♦ Small signals to "bring them back" and focus (e.g., a tap on the desk)

Assignments

♦ Provide a peer tutor to help write down assignments or take notes

♦ Send home a weekly list of missed assignments (by U.S. mail or email)

- Allow bulleting of answers instead of full sentences
- Give time
- Do major assignments in small pieces

Physical Environment

- Let students work standing up, lying down, sitting cross-legged on the floor, sprawled across the desk so that they feel comfortable (but *not* disruptive)
- Laugh, have fun, be playful
- Seat students up front and maintain proximity
- Seat students in the back so that they can get up and walk around without distracting others

Self-Monitoring

- Teach self-talk skills
- Have older students learn to write notes to themselves
- Help students set goals, then conference to see whether they have met them
- Allow for an escape valve—let students get up and move, leave the room, walk around the halls
- Encourage self-reporting and self-monitoring
- Help students feel comfortable seeking help
- Ask students what will help; they are the experts about how they learn best

Giving Directions

- Simplify commands and avoid giving multiple commands
- Repeat directions if necessary
- Make lists for students to refer to
- Communicate with parents (*don't* expect notes given to students to arrive home)

- Remember that every day is a new day

- Keep folders at your desk for important information students
  need (*don't* expect them to be responsible for saving important
  papers)

- Help with locker or desk clean outs

Is there one specific thing to do that will help all ADHD students?
Absolutely not. The storytellers simply ask that you validate their
being and try something. It doesn't have to be one big fight after
another. Brandon can go get his book; Kari can walk around the
room; Jennie can sit in the front; Geoff can be late with an assignment. In the end, their teachers slowly helped these students figure
out those strategies that worked to help them make sense of the
world.

Using any of the techniques just listed won't ensure that your frustration level will change and that the student will suddenly be successful. But, sometimes you will succeed and you will certainly be
sending a message to the student that he or she is worth it. If nothing
else, that message of worth means you've done something of importance in your classroom.

Insights From Teachers

Acceptance, Awareness, and Humor

Anne Snell teaches in an urban high school in southern California. She has been teaching for seventeen years. The following is a summary of her experiences and some suggestions to help students. (Note: The names of students in this essay have been changed.)

On the first day of school in the fall, the first names I learn are those of my ADHD students. They often call attention to themselves simply by the way they tumble into the room. By the second day of school, I'm commiserating with myself about the number of ADHD students, diagnosed or not, that I have during the day; three in period one, one in period two, two in period three, and so forth. A high number means that pens and pencils will disappear all year at an alarming rate and that I will talk about certain classes with the inexorable refrain, "That class is driving me crazy." It means that I will have to apologize more to students when I become impatient; that I will have to dig into my bag of strategies, knowing that what works one week may not work the next, and that what works for one student may not work for another.

I also know that I will have to work incredibly hard to create a classroom environment in which every student feels safe; because of their disruptive behavior, ADHD students are often the target of angry comments from others in the class. Oddly, by the end of the year, ADHD students are often my favorites because I've spent the most time and energy on them. I know them the best.

I've learned that there is nothing permanent to learn about how to deal with ADHD students. There is nothing that I can apply 100 percent of the time with 100 percent success for 100 percent of my ADHD students. But I do recognize that 100 percent of the time I need to build relationships with the students, so I can hear what they are telling me about how they best learn and so that they can trust me to guide them on the path to learning.

I focus on three attitudes to provide better success for these students, better access to the curriculum, and a more comfortable classroom environment: acceptance, awareness, and humor. First, I use acceptance. I accept that a particular class will be more difficult than the others, or that two classes will be more difficult, or three; or that the year will be more difficult than other years. I accept that there will be more noise in a particular class and that noise is OK. I always try to remember that my goal is not silence, but learning. If learning is not occurring, I assess the reasons and change my teaching strategies. I accept that my ADHD students will probably take more of my time than the other students. I always try to remember that these students are innocent, that I wouldn't discriminate against a student because of eyesight, and I should not discriminate against a student because of a neural difference. Most important, I accept the students for who they are and meet them where they are.

Second, I use awareness. I listen to what my ADHD students tell me. Sometimes they tell me with words; sometimes with behavior. For example, in tenth-grade English, Tyler sat next to his best friend and talked constantly in a low voice. To stop the talking, I moved him to a new desk. Tyler's talking became louder, his movements more pronounced. So I moved him again. And again. At each new desk, Tyler became the center of an increasingly louder whirlwind. In assessing the situation, I realized that when he had been sitting next to his close friend, he at least had talked quietly and his movements had been minimal. His behavior was telling me something, so I asked Tyler whether he'd like to move back to his original seat. He said yes, that his friend helped him focus. I moved him and allowed the conversations to go on. I told them both that I wanted them to talk softly, to be aware of the students around them, and to try to focus on what we were doing. With other modifications, Tyler was able to pass tenth-grade English. It was the first time he'd ever passed an English class.

Rodrigo was in my ninth-grade English class. Those English classes are limited to twenty students; hence, a number of desks were empty in the back of my room. During the first two weeks of school, I had to continually remind Rodrigo to sit in his regular desk. Finally, I asked him whether it helped him to sit in different desks. He said that sometimes he learned better in different places, and that sometimes he just needed to move. I gave him a permanent pass to leave the room for a walk to the water fountain, and I told him to sit wherever he thought he would learn the best. Sometimes he sat in his regular desk; sometimes he moved himself to the back of the room; sometimes he sat at the corner table. Occasionally, when working independently on an assignment, he would turn a desk to the wall. Over the course of the year, three other students did the same thing; in fact, for the final exam in the spring, five students wanted to face the wall.

My favorite moment with Rodrigo occurred in the spring when he came into the room with a friend. The friend asked where he sat. Rodrigo looked around a little puzzled, then smiled and flung out his arms to encompass the entire room. "These are all my desks," he said. "I sit everywhere." I've always remembered that moment. As a teacher, I felt good that Rodrigo felt safe in my classroom.

A few years later Claire joined me for ninth-grade English. She was loud, disruptive, and full of attitude. On the phone with her mother early in the year, I heard Claire yelling in the background. I asked if I might speak with her. I asked Claire to help me come up with some ideas that might remind her not to shout out in class. We finally settled on the idea of putting something on her desk as a reminder. When I suggested a beanie baby, she agreed immediately. We ran through a long list of animals and finally settled on a parrot. I brought it in for her on the following Monday. When Claire shouted out of turn, I would say, "Pick up your parrot." It was a gentle way to remind her to stop disrupting the class. The parrot worked for about two months—the disruptions were about a fourth of what they had been. Claire had to take second-semester English 9 in summer school because she failed it, but we'd managed to keep her in the classroom, and she felt safe.

Avery was a student who talked and questioned constantly. He shouted out answers to every single question, answered questions before I was finished posing them, and walked into the classroom every day asking mundane question after mundane question. In desperation, I typed up a note to put on his desk. It said, "You may speak only five times during class. Make sure that what you say is important to you." There were five boxes for him to check off. The strategy worked for quite awhile, and I was able to remind him to stop disrupting by simply asking him to check off one of his boxes. Later, I asked him to help me post a "Raise Your Hand" policy statement with reasons why it would help the class. It was, of course, geared toward his behavior. He came up with the reasons for the policy and explained them to the class. Although he was never able to raise his hand without much grunting and arm waving, he did try.

Christopher had trouble focusing on multistep projects in a creative writing class. He often came up to my desk to work so that I could give him directions step-by-step rather than all at once. Being aware of his problems helped me focus on the solution.

Caleb forgot a book report at home, so I asked him to call his mother from my room so that she could post a note by the door to remind him to bring it the next day. I didn't take points off because it was late. I treat students differently because I want to treat them fairly. If another student says that this doesn't seem fair, I simply say that some students need more time and others don't, or that some students only need to do half the assignment and others don't. Not one student has ever argued with me about that issue.

Not only do I try to be aware of what my ADHD students are telling me, but I also try to help students become aware of who they are and how they learn. I want them to become self-reflective so that they can learn to advocate for themselves with other teachers.

What helps me survive most of all is the third attitude, humor. I can get angry or I can laugh. I choose to do the latter. Pencils are always an issue in my classroom. I have a can of them on my desk and they disappear quickly. One year I decided to wire artificial flowers on the top of the pencils so that when students started to put them in their backpacks they would have the reminder that the pencil belonged in my room. It was amusing to look out over the classroom and see big strong teenaged boys writing with flowers. It was even more amusing to watch the students with ADHD slowly, methodically, and without even thinking, dismantle the flowers until all that was left were a few wire strands at the top of the pencil. I could have gotten mad at them for ruining the flowers. I could have refused to let them use the pencils at all. Instead, I chose humor and the learning continued.

Then there is the story of the clipboard. One year my ninth-grade English students were assigned to interview people outside of class and make a chart of their findings for use in a presentation. Providing a clipboard to each group seemed to get the groups excited. However, one group hadn't started on their interviews a week later. As I tried to encourage and help them understand what was required, one ADHD student in the group was bending the group's clipboard back and forth, back and forth, back and forth. I finished my pep talk about the same time the clipboard snapped in two. Without missing a beat, and not even aware that he'd just destroyed the clipboard, the student said, "Could you lend us a clipboard?" I simply said, "Yes" and was happy when the group came in two days later ready for their presentation—chart and all. I could have gotten angry that he broke the clipboard. That would not have helped. Instead, I kept my humor intact and we went on with the learning process.

The issue of medication frequently comes up. Should we or should we not medicate the child? In meetings with parents about ADHD students, I do my best to focus on the cognitive growth I see in these students. Although it is not my place to make a recommendation for or against medication, I explain to parents as honestly as I can how their child's lack of ability to focus is affecting his or her intellectual growth.

Sometimes when a child is put on medication in the middle of the year, parents have asked me whether I see a difference. Again, it is not my place to take a position for or against medication. It is my place to explain the differences I see so that parents can make a decision in consultation with their family doctor. I always try to let both parents and students know that what I'm interested in is not a mellow classroom environment, but rather a chance for the student to learn. Decisions about medication should be made not because a teacher wants a quiet classroom, but because each student has a right to optimal intellectual development.

ADHD students are a challenge, but I've learned over the years that it is the challenging students who often make me feel the most fulfilled and who keep me teaching year after year. They have a right to our highest and most dedicated effort.

Keep Your Kindness

Peggy Sullivan has been a middle school teacher for twenty years. For two years, she served as the Teacher-in-Residence in a college teacher education program. Peggy said that she began her career as a traditionalist—kids sitting in rows, hands folded on desks, no talking in the halls. By recognizing the needs of her students, she began to change her classroom practices. I had the opportunity to interview Peggy about her teaching beliefs, about students, and about ADHD.

Twenty years ago when I started teaching I was almost the exact opposite of what I am today. The driving force for changing my classroom practice was recognizing the needs of my students. Now I identify the needs of children and accommodate them the best I can. I want teachers to understand that change is healthy. Change is needed when the demands of the children warrant the change. We have to change.

I don't look at an ADHD child and say, "This is an ADHD child." I say, "This is Johnny and he's challenged with ADHD." Every child who is challenged with ADHD is different from every other child who is challenged with ADHD. When I have children with ADHD in my room, the first thing I do is find out the ways that they learn best. I get to know the children. I have conversations with them, listen to them, and find out what they like to do before and after school, what their favorite subject is. I don't think of them as different. Every child is different and unique and delightful, so I get to know Johnny and I find out what he's about as I do with all the children.

I am always available to my students. I'm in my classroom early and sometimes I stay late. Sometimes I go outside with the children after lunch. We take walks around the school. The children at lunch tell you things that you don't even want to know. If we're accessible to the children and we listen and we remember what they tell us, we can get to know them really well.

The school environment is not always conducive to learning. Teachers need to make sure that the physical environment meets the needs of the children. I cannot sit still in a class for fifty to sixty minutes straight without getting up, and I'm old and mature and self-disciplined. The classroom environment should accommodate the children. The children should not be pounded into conformity to fit the classroom environment.

Students have total freedom of movement in my classroom. They can get up and go to the back of the room, quietly jog in place, quietly do jumping jacks, or just pace. They're still listening; they're still involved; and they'll still raise their hands, respond, and interact. Some children benefit from bungee cords that are attached to the front of a desk so they can pump their feet. It's very quiet and not distracting. It's all a matter of getting your environment to support learning. It's ridiculous that we ask children to sit in a chair or on a carpet for forty minutes, making sure their bottoms are flat and their legs are folded.

There are other freedoms in my classroom. When my children need something, they don't have to ask permission to get it. They need paper, they know where it is. There's only one drawer in the teacher's desk they cannot go into. But they can go get a pencil, a pen, an eraser, paper clips, a stapler, a glue stick—whatever. They can get up and use the electric pencil sharpener. It's their home away from home; it's their workplace.

I talk to the kids. I ask them, "You're struggling with this. How can I help you? How can we do this better so that you really feel that you're gaining ground here?" Believe it or not, if children trust the adult that's asking them, trust that the teacher is not going to hurt them with some kind of negative body language response, verbal abuse, or sarcasm; if they feel that this adult really loves them, they'll tell you. Classroom management is an issue sometimes because children are in there fighting for their lives against the adult who has all the power. Teachers are powerful people. We need to watch how we use our power.

I teach craftsmanship and pride in the work that they do. I don't give homework. We do OT—overtime. If a child needs to take work home because she wants the work to be good, she asks me, "Can I bring this home and work on it?" There's work that I will not allow them to take home because I don't want it damaged or lost or eaten by the dog, or have baby brother spit up on it. They'll work on it with me during help-class. I don't believe in homework for many content areas; the one definite exception is math. Children need to practice that independently for understanding. I believe children should be able to decide when they need extra time, to take work home. That's the way it works, and the children make the decision.

My students challenged with ADHD don't seem to have more difficulty taking a task to the perfection that I expect. They aren't sloppier and they don't tend to rush through work. I think that's because I believe in them. They know what they're capable of and they want to see improvement. They know I'll support them.

One fellow in particular was significantly challenged with ADHD. He always produced wonderful work for me. What motivated him was pride in the outcome. He knew what he could do; he knew what he wanted it to look like when he was finished; and when he held it up and it was a wonderful piece of work, he knew he had managed himself through the entire process. When we genuinely appreciate and recognize what children do, they will do so much more the next time.

When children with ADHD feel accepted, their stress decreases, which increases their ability to do quality work and decreases their disruptive behavior. When they have a sufficient level of comfort with their learning environment, the behavioral issues seem to decrease. We know that a hostile work environment decreases adults' productivity. It's the same for kids; a hostile school environment reduces productivity.

I give instruction in a way that empowers children to participate. My students love to choose and help me plan. When we were doing the Civil War unit, I said to them:

> Okay we've come right up to 1860. Lincoln's been elected. We know the war's going to just burst forth any day now, so here's the deal, ladies and gentlemen. This is the decision we have to make. Do we continue with the war and get to 1865, or do we put the war on the back burner and begin our civil rights unit now? The civil rights unit's events began in 1865 with the birth of the Klan and we're going to go right up to today. Which way do you think it's going to work better?

So I gave them a few minutes to chat amongst themselves, and even left the room so they could feel free to just yakety-yak. I came back in and took a vote. We needed a two-thirds majority because this was a big decision. It was just about unanimous; they had really come to a consensus. They wanted to do the civil rights unit first.

When we finished the civil rights unit, I asked them, "Well, what do you think now that we've completed the civil rights unit, how do you feel?" The overall consensus was that they had made a good decision. They all felt they understood the Civil War much better having taken that side trip with the civil rights unit. They were very proud of their decision. They were invested and they were making some big choices.

There's an ownership quality to my instruction and I do that on purpose. It makes my job of fulfilling their needs easier because they are invested in it. The instruction is a partnership between the students and me. I change my instruction with each group that sits in my room. I can't do it the same when the children are different.

My children know I care for them. It's ongoing. It's being genuine. I was scolding one group of kids about something and telling them how disappointed I was. I made it short and quick. I didn't prolong it and it was done. And one of my young men looked up and blurted right out of his mouth, "We're sorry Ms. S., but we know you still love us." They know. They can tell you the adults that genuinely care about them and the adults that don't and just pretend that they do.

There's one young gentleman who was very, very significantly challenged by ADHD, struggled all the way through school, and is probably struggling right now in high school. He was so resented because of his behavior. I don't think it was something he plotted and planned; I think it was just a survival instinct. School had just batted him around emotionally and psychologically so horribly that his behavior had become a real issue. When I was with him, however, he was a perfect gentleman, he was very cooperative, he worked well with the other children, and he was very proud of his work. He got a very good grade in my class.

One day, I was coming down the corridor and he was with another teacher in the hall. He was behaving so abominably to the other teacher that I was completely taken aback. I had never seen this child behave that way and this was two-thirds into the school year. I was so shocked that I just walked up to him and stood there aghast. I didn't even say anything, I just looked at him. He stopped dead when I walked up and he looked at me with such an awful look that I had caught him behaving like that. He just looked into my face and said, "I am so sorry." Why did he behave for me? He knew I thought he was wonderful and capable. I believed in him and, in my class, he believed in himself.

I welcome all children into my classroom and I love them all. They're partners with me. They trust me. They know I'm not going to hurt them, not on purpose. But I'm strict. My expectations are: "You will be ladies and gentlemen in my room. We treat each other with respect"; and that is what they do.

One thing I firmly believe is that every single teacher, or any adult who provides direct services to children, should always ask, "How would I feel if I were this child's mom or dad?" There needs to be a strong identification with the parents, almost as a coparent. I firmly believe in close contact with parents. There are some parents who I call every Friday afternoon before I leave my building; they need all the help they can get.

The children are wonderful, all of them. They're all such sweeties. We need to start looking at them as individuals.

What I would like to say to teachers and anyone else who works directly with children, particularly those with ADHD, is "Keep your kindness and don't damage them." That's it in a nutshell.

Medication

My Eyes Are Metal and the Teacher is a Magnet

No book that deals with Attention Deficit/Hyperactivity Disorder (ADHD) would be complete without a discussion about medication as a treatment option. The use of stimulant medication has led to much controversy. On the one hand are those who feel that drugs are overprescribed and used as a way to simply subdue children. On the other hand are those who benefit from medications' use—the children, and the parents and teachers who live with them day after day.

If you doubt the efficacy of using medication, listen to Brandon and his mom talk about how the medication helped him. Brandon's mom said this after he started on medication.

> The kindergarten teacher, the one he had all the trouble with, saw this little boy sitting in the chair and she didn't know who he was. She said Brandon never sat still long enough for her to see his back. She actually saw what it was like to go from the worst child to the best child because of the medication. He does need it. You can see a difference.

Brandon agreed, "When it wears off I really can't pay attention and I can't sit still. Then I just can't do anything."

Or ask Grant and Belkies who have both seen positive results with the medication. Grant took Ritalin throughout high school. "After I started taking Ritalin I was able to keep my focus on something for more than fifteen minutes. It helped." Belkies began taking Ritalin in college, and said: "I can see the difference. I know when I am not taking it. It is easier to focus when I am taking the medicine."

It appears counterintuitive to use stimulants on children who are already overactive. The medications seem to work by stimulating neural pathways—areas of the brain—that control impulse and concentration, arousing them. This results in an increased ability for individuals to control behavior and concentrate on tasks.

The use of stimulant medication to treat overactivity has been around for almost seventy years. In 1937, Dr. Charles Bradley noticed that the stimulants he was using to treat children with emotional disturbances seemed to decrease overactive behaviors. Building on the work of Bradley, about fifteen years later, Ritalin (methylphenidate) was developed and became an accepted treatment for hyperactivity. Today stimulant medications, such as Ritalin, Adderall, and Concerta, are the most widely used medications to treat ADHD.

During the past three decades, the use of stimulant medication to treat ADHD has increased dramatically. It is estimated that between 2 to 2.5 million children in schools today take some kind of medication to help them deal with the effects of ADHD *(www.cdc.gov* 2003).

Academic success requires the ability to organize the environment, to attend to directions, and to focus on tasks long enough to complete them. That often requires holding three or four ideas in the mind at one time. Success may require sitting still, paying attention, and waiting for your turn. ADHD students are at high risk for failure in the classroom. Should they take medication to help them achieve success?

The answer is complicated. Medications are not useful for everyone. Educators and parents must ask themselves some questions:

◆ Will medication help students organize, attend, focus, and wait?

◆ Will taking medication help students feel success at school?

◆ Will it help them think at higher levels?

◆ Will medication help them learn the skills they will need as adults?

◆ Will it help them to make sense of their lives?

Should medication be denied if it could help? No one would do that for other physical conditions, and it should not be denied to students with ADHD. When carefully monitored by a doctor who is knowledgeable about ADHD, medications can become the key to success at school. Medication has been known to help those with ADHD focus their attention, control their overactivity, become less impulsive, and be able to engage in high-level tasks.

Medications do not cure the root cause of the ADHD, just as insulin is not a cure for diabetes. They simply allow the child to gain some success in school by helping him or her focus on tasks. As a report from Children and Adults with Attention Deficit Disorder (CHADD) said:

"Medication does not cure ADHD; when effective, it alleviates ADHD symptoms during the time it is active" (*www.chadd.org*, p. 3).

Are some medications overprescribed? That question is not the concern of the classroom teacher. Certainly, medications have been shown to help a vast number of students who struggle because of ADHD. The role of the teacher is to help identify behaviors so that parents can work with physicians to find the best treatment for their children.

Listen to Their Stories

Some of the storytellers took medication continuously, some from time to time, and some chose not to take any. Their stories can help us to understand the effect that taking medication had on their behavior and success in school. Listening to their stories can facilitate understanding of the role of medication as a treatment option for students with ADHD. It is not the educators' place to judge whether medication should be used or not; it's not even their job to suggest it as an option. It is, however, important to work with students and their parents to identify behaviors and to give feedback to doctors about changes in behavior. That's why you need to hear their stories.

Kari's Story

Kari is the perfect example of a child who benefited from taking medication so much that she made a believer out of her teacher. Kari started taking Adderall in the second grade. It wasn't an easy decision for the family to put their second grader on a highly controlled medication. The results have been worth it though. Listen to her mom.

We finally decided in January of second grade to try medication because she was just all over the place and she wasn't doing as well as she could academically. So she started medication the middle of second grade and there was a dramatic difference at school. Her teacher, at this point, was really not in favor of medication. The first day Kari was on medication, the teacher commented to me that this is one of the kids who so clearly benefits from being on medication.

We really struggled at home. She's kind of a skinny kid and she lost close to ten pounds. She would come home from school and wouldn't have eaten a thing out of her lunchbox all day. We tried to cut down her Adderall. She was doing well on 10 mgs so we went to 7.5 mgs with the doctor's suggestion. And immediately she knew that wasn't working for her. She went to school that day and came home and said, 'I need to take my ten pill.' All she heard all day long was 'blah, blah, blah, blah, blah, blah.' And she said, 'When I take my ten pill I feel like my eyes are metal and the teacher is a magnet.' The medication helps her that much to pay attention.

Finding the correct medication and dosage is an ongoing struggle and an important part of a treatment plan. Loss of appetite and insomnia are two of the most common side effects of stimulant medications. Kari's parents decided to try her on Concerta due to the loss of appetite on the Adderall. Her mom had this to say about changing the medication and having to use it at all.

We tried her on Concerta at the end of the year hoping that her appetite might be better. As she came off of the Concerta, she would just be explosive at home—almost aggressive and angry. We saw a real rebound effect with the Concerta which we didn't expect. So we kind of reluctantly put her back on Adderall and gave her meals at seven or eight at night before she'd go to bed. We made milkshakes for breakfast if that's what she was willing to drink. So her weight has been stable and she's sleeping a little bit better.

The first few weeks that she was on it she was in the nurse's office all the time. I think that she felt different and wasn't sure what it was. If she has somewhere to go to, or a playdate where she needs to focus, we give it to her on the weekend. She'll say sometimes, 'I don't want to take my pills because it's not me, it's not the happy-go-lucky me.' That's the part we don't want to lose—the bubbly part. She is this very gregarious kid and we don't want to lose that.

She clearly brings herself to your attention when she's not on medication. Kari will have her stuff in every single room of this house. At the end of the day you can walk through the house and her stuff is everywhere. It's unbelievable. The first week she was on medication, she and I went upstairs together and cleaned her room. It was like a gift because she could spend some time and put her books back in the bookcase and put some things away. I think the medication has really helped the hyperactivity part.

I was so upset having to put her on medication. I think seeing the difference, so dramatically, so quickly, made us realize she does need to be on medication; we just need to figure out what's the right one for her.

Kari clearly saw the effects of taking the medication. She commented:

It seems a lot easier to follow my teachers and what they're saying instead of going off into the distance and daydreaming. At first having ADD was pretty frightening because I didn't know what was going to happen. When I took my medication, I worried that I was going to be a completely different person. How am I supposed to take this pill if I'd never swallowed one? It just seems that it's changed my life a lot. I don't think I'm as active as I used to be. I can't eat as much as I could. I lost a lot of weight and can't get to sleep or get up in the morning. I haven't forgotten my medicine at all this year. Last year my teacher could really notice when I forgot. She noticed that I was "out" a lot and couldn't really concentrate on her.

How Other Storytellers Reacted to Medication

Geoff's mom remembers the day that he took medication (Adderall) for the first time. "He thought he had been born again. The way he puts it is, 'I can finish a thought.'" Geoff described that day and how he feels when taking medication.

The first day I took it, I read whatever we needed to read and remembered it and I was like, "Whoa, this is amazing." I read the entire book cover to cover without skipping any chapters, which is something I'd never done, at all—ever. I've just been taking it ever since.

I'm happy with it. I wouldn't have considered myself to have been organized, my whole life organized until I went on the Adderall.

I don't want to be taking this stuff for the rest of my life. My thinking is, if I can get myself into a rhythm, get myself organized, just be comfortable with that and just live that way then I don't see how I could need it anymore. Maybe the quick fix isn't the best thing, but I've also learned to think of taking a drug as just helping me from point A to B, and I feel comfortable with that.

Marti said that her son Alex had a similar reaction when he took medication for the first time. He had to take a test.

> He was quite desperate to do well. He took one of the pills and I went out somewhere that night. When I got back around 10:30, he had his stuff at the dining room table, all organized. He must have talked to me for about forty-five minutes about how excited he was. He knew the information, everything connected, everything made sense. He could not believe how he was able to concentrate. It was a miracle and he aced the final.
>
> After that experience it sort of opened his eyes, and one of the things he told the psychiatrist after he started on a prescription was how he couldn't believe how much it helped his painting. He would come to some kind of technical impasse, and he said in the past what he would do is just throw it aside and go back to it later. But now, with the medication, he actually works through the problem. So he's been on the medication but in spite of the medication, he still exhibits symptoms, forgetting this and not getting to that.

Marti's third son, Nick, also tried medication. He wasn't as successful. Although it did help him focus, his loss of appetite and insomnia bothered him. Over the next few years, he tried a couple of different types of medication. They all worked for awhile, but eventually it was as though his body got used to the medications and they stopped being effective.

So, you see, medication is not a miracle cure. For about 80 percent of people diagnosed with ADHD, medication might be effective. Even with those 80 percent, treatment for ADHD has to be combined with other strategies for helping students learn to cope in the world.

Kristina was initially against medication but tried it and saw how much she benefited from it:

> I like it. Concentration level is really there. It's a huge change being in class, hearing a lecture. I don't get confused anymore and a lot of things are more understandable in all my classes. One side effect I just realized last week, kind of a downfall, is social anxiety. When I'm taking it, it's harder for me to interact and socialize with all my peers, but I'm comfortable talking to adults. When I'm not on it, I can interact and socialize with my peers and it's harder to talk to adults. It's like it all gets swapped around. Taking it, I get very calm, very mellow, and really focused on school.

I forgot to bring my medication to school once. It was harder to focus in class. I was more hyper, more energetic—yelling, screaming, and running around with everybody.

I was against Ritalin. I didn't like the idea of something that could have so much control over someone. It kind of frightened me. I had tried a lot of other things. A therapist had taught me some breathing exercises and kind of like a holistic approach to things, but I found that it was actually hard to remember to do the breathing exercises. I tried a lot of different things before I decided to take medication.

In her story, Jennie mentioned that although medication helped her, she noticed that sometimes she focused on the wrong things. "It helps you focus, but you've got to make sure that your attention goes to the right thing because if it doesn't, you're so going to be stuck on something else." She said, "I feel like when I take it I focus in so tight on one thing that nothing else is in my view. If you can get focused on the right thing, you're golden. But if you can't, you're so in trouble because you don't see anything else."

Nicholas noticed a similar effect. "With the medication, it got me to focus but not necessarily on school. I've been fanatical about cars, reading car magazines, and car classifieds, so I wouldn't necessarily buckle down on schoolwork. But I'd sit down and do what interested me, which usually wasn't school." He also said, "It didn't hinder me. It may have even helped a little bit. It wasn't a miracle drug." Nicholas had been taking some sort of medication off and on since the fourth grade. He is medication free now.

Jillian noticed changes in her behavior with the medication. "I didn't like the medication to begin with. It changed me; it made me not the person I was; I wasn't random; I wasn't fun; I wasn't hyper when I wanted to be. I wasn't always in a good mood but I was concentrated and I was focused." She went on to say this about one experience while on medication:

I was a horrible runner in cross-country then I started Adderall. It improved my motivation and concentration. It was unbelievable, I got most-improved, which is why I am so dedicated to cross-country; and I got voted captain, which I never thought of before. Being diagnosed with ADD, I never thought I'd ever be the captain of anything. I'm kind of happy with where I am and it's all kind of good.

Physicians, parents, and those with ADHD are the ones who should make decisions about medication. Constant communication with teachers is an important part of the physician's work to find an effective medication.

Rob also saw the positive effects of the medication. "I'm just more focused on what I'm doing." But he went on to say, "I was medicated for the sole purpose of getting through school, which seems a little messed up to me. Now what do I do that I need to pay attention to?" He stopped taking medication after he graduated from high school.

Would medication be necessary if classrooms were designed to meet the needs of diverse learners? Can teachers create environments in which students' activity, impulsivity, and lack of attention are not seen as problems to be solved but characteristics to work with? And after appropriate environments for learning have been created, will medication help stimulate neural pathways and make the world a bit clearer?

Everyone owes it to students to give them all possible options for success. Sometimes that means the use of medication, which is a serious and complicated decision that must be made in consultation with a physician who knows a lot about ADHD. If parents choose not to use medications, the role of the teacher does not change. You still work with every child who comes through the classroom door, letting them all know that whatever their specific needs, you will work with them to create a learning environment for success.

Jessie's Story

This Wasn't Supposed to Be My Life

Jessie was twenty one when I interviewed her in a small cafe two blocks from her apartment in Boston, Massachusetts. She was finishing her fourth year in college, working for a BFA in acting. She was going to spend the fall semester in Los Angeles with the school and graduate in December.

Jessie was not diagnosed with ADHD until her sophomore year in college. You can tell from her story, however, that she has struggled her whole life. Listen to what she says about living with the challenges of ADHD.

This wasn't supposed to be my life. This is not supposed to be hard for me. I just get so frustrated, like why is this happening? It just feels like injustice to have to go through all that I went through. I just didn't feel like it was fair. I'm supposed to be smart, why is this so hard for me? I always had that part of me that was like, "This isn't really my fault." I knew there was something else and it wasn't me.

In terms of school and even life, I was always very interested in everything but my attention span was everywhere. One of my parents' friends once bet me a dollar that I couldn't sit still for a minute. I lost. I thought I was going to win. I was so sure. It was never a matter of not wanting to be doing what I was doing. It was just that if it went on too long I couldn't handle it. I like to talk. I like to explore things.

Elementary School

I was in Montessori School until the third grade. I got in trouble for talking even in Montessori school, which is where you're supposed to be able to talk. In the Montessori school, I guess I didn't ever think about excelling because I just loved working in my math workbook because it was like games, like little puzzles. It was like play time.

After the third grade, I moved and went to a small private school. I liked the curriculum but there were a couple teachers that hated me. One of them called me a brat. It was just that I was talkative. I talked a lot because that's what I wanted to do. I didn't like to sit and listen to somebody talk for a very long time. But I never did badly in academics.

I moved to the public school and my third- and fourth-grade teachers were amazing. We did little things for a half hour the whole day so that was perfect for me. We would read a story for half an hour and then do a little science project for a half hour and that kind of curriculum setup was perfect. I didn't have to listen to anyone talk for more than forty-five minutes. In fifth grade, kids started making fun of me for talking. I had the reputation of being loud and talkative.

I was always big into learning and I got frustrated when teachers didn't see that about me. They would say, "Oh, you're a troublemaker. You don't care about anything." It was because I would be talking or daydreaming. Once I drew this really beautiful drawing in pencil on my desk and got in trouble for it. I was listening and paying attention, but it was just helpful to do something else at the same time.

Sixth grade was when I started to lose it with academics. It was the class setup. We'd be in class for forty-five minutes or an hour all sitting in rows, listening to a lecture and we'd have to read from a textbook and that just wasn't my thing at all. The teacher didn't have time to work individually with me on something because there were thirty-five kids in a class. If I couldn't talk about it with somebody, I didn't learn about it.

I think I got most of my assignments in on time. I made it a habit of telling my parents what was due and when it was due so they could be my check up. They could say, "Did you hand that in?" And I would think, "Oh, I haven't done that yet. I have to do it really fast." I got in trouble for talking and daydreaming and being kind of an airhead in class, but I was always doing the work.

In seventh and eighth grade, I went to a professional performing arts school. My teacher for acting and musical theater didn't like me because I was too talkative and too disruptive and I was too bouncing off the walls and she could never find me. She would be like, "Oh I can't deal with you. You're too much right now." Half the teachers were really trying to help me with that and the other half were just like, "No, she's just a crazy kid."

Once I got put in the corner for talking during class. I pulled my arms and legs into my shirt and was sitting perched on the chair. I fell forward and I smashed my face on the ground. It was kind of funny—that was my ADD thing—to find something fun to do. One teacher came over and said, "Oh, my God, this is terrible." The other teacher said, "Serves her right for talking in class." Some teachers just shouldn't be teachers.

High School: I Wanted to Fit In Finally

High school work was horrible. I would cry every day. Come home, have to write a paper, read a chapter in my history book. My mom would sit there and have to read it to me and after every paragraph she would say, "What did I just say?" and half the time I would be like, "I don't know. I have no idea what you just said." Half a line would get out and I would stop listening. It was like I would have to go word by word and process it like a little tiny puzzle that you put together and it was frustrating.

I felt very out of place because nobody really understood and I didn't really understand myself. I was always an outcast because I was really smart but at the same time I wasn't. I was kind of an airhead and people were baffled by the fact that I was actually smart. That sort of made me have an identity crisis. Once I got to high school I sort of latched on to the fact that I was a pretty girl and went in that direction, which totally screwed everything up.

I went to supposedly the best high school on the East Coast. I passed the test to get in and then I was stuck in a school that was terrible for me. The kids were supposed to be smart so they didn't need the extra help that most kids needed. It was like we can just give these kids a textbook and talk for forty-five minutes and they'll be fine and that was what smart was. That's not the kind of smart I was, so I did terrible. I did great in English classes because they were based on discussion. History classes and science classes were the worst. I would try and listen.

Before every semester I would have my little notebook with the dividers and the colored pens and be real excited about taking notes and then I would pass notes in class all the time and not pay attention. I just couldn't stay with it because there was no reason for me to be learning that. I remember in my history class I raised my hand to ask a question and he said that we didn't have time for discussion. Most of the time it was just lecture and we listened and then we had assignments from the book. There was nothing creative about it.

Later in high school I went to a school that was supposed to be for kids who don't work in the typical structured environment but the problem was that it was all kids who don't work in the typical structured environment and my ADD focused on the kids rather than the learning. I just went further down the road that they were going on and I got involved in everything that they were doing. I started smoking pot and I started drinking. I had never done anything like that before. It was not in my world. I didn't do badly in my academics but I didn't know what to do. I was following whatever because I was made fun of so much for being who I was and I just didn't want to do that anymore. I wanted to fit in finally.

They made fun of me because I wasn't like them. It was just like I was weird. In the fourth grade, I had come home and told my dad that a guy in school called me a four-eyed skinny bean pole and my dad said, "What do you think about that?" and I said, "Well it's true."

The math class that I had was one of my favorite classes. I loved it. What we did was we could go out, like there is a building in New York that is triangular shaped and we would have to figure out the volume of the building using little tools like a straw and a protractor, go measuring the steps we took from it. We would have to find the width of the river by doing the same thing, cosine, tangent, and all that stuff, and we started every class with a math riddle so it was more hands-on, going out to the world and trying it.

What made me feel good about myself was doing well—accomplishing things in my life. I think the one thing that saved me from really going off the edge was the plays that I did. I felt good doing it. I could say, "I can do this," and people applaud when I'm done. They don't say, "What the hell is she doing? She can't do that."

I made a choice. I did not want my life to go like this. I went back to the first high school—the one that was supposed to be so good. "I can't mess up." I thought. Everybody says I can't do it. That was a lot of the draw too, people saying you can't do this and so I say, "Yes I can." That was a lot of it and I made it through.

College

I was diagnosed halfway through college. College was tough. The beginning was hard. I was away and I was free and doing all this stuff. I had a million different jobs and having so much fun. And my classes, I could just sleep through them; there was nobody to tell me to go. I remember my mom would drag me out of bed every morning for high school.

In college, the classes I had with a lot of friends I would go to because they were fun and my friends would be going so I'd just go with them. There was one class I got a D in. I got there ten minutes late because I had to walk across campus. I sat in the back and fell asleep. My teacher was really nice and didn't fail me which I totally deserved. It was just that there wasn't anything about it that made me feel that I should be learning it. In college, the shortest classes were an hour and fifteen minutes. For me, forty-five minutes was unbearable. You have all this reading to do. I never had time.

I got diagnosed when I spent a semester in Europe. I made a decision to get every single piece of work done, every reading assignment. Before I never did reading assignments. I would peruse them in class and pick up what other people said. I remember one night I was sitting in the lounge where everybody would sit and do their work and everybody was gone. I was still sitting there with an assignment, poring over it, doing the same thing that my mom and I would have to do, picking it through word by word because it's intense stuff that's really complicated and I was crying, "I have to do this. I can't give up." My friend who has ADD came downstairs and said, "I'm really not supposed to do this but I can tell you have something that's going on here because this shouldn't happen to somebody who's smart and I know you're smart." So she gave me an Adderall and she said, "Try it and see how it works and if it works, go to the doctor."

It was amazing. I was understanding what I was reading. I was making notes in the margins. There is something about putting it together in my mind and keeping focus on what's happening rather than what's happening everywhere. I went to a doctor the next day and she talked to me and said, "This is not a big thing in Europe but from your description it sounds good." All they had there was Ritalin and I started taking it and I noticed a difference.

One thing I noticed was at dinner. Everything was set up, napkins, forks, plates, cups. We'd get it all and go to the table. Before I started the Ritalin I would get a cup and a plate and go to my chair. And I'd go back and get silverware and then go back and get a salt packet and then I gotta get a napkin and I'd be walking back and forth from the table about ten times. After a week or two of the Ritalin, I realized that I was less and less disorganized and more and more focused on what I had to do and I would remember what assignments were due what day.

Since then I've just been doing amazingly well in school. It sort of gave me permission to not be a bad kid. I realized that it was no longer cool to do bad in school. My junior year I made a decision to do as well as I could. Last semester I got straight As.

I take Adderall now. I sometimes feel that if I'm not doing something when I take the Adderall there's something wrong. I can't allow myself to just sit on the couch and watch TV. I have to make phone calls, or organize my socks, or put everything in alphabetical order in my bookshelf.

My friends can tell. They'll say, "You took your medicine today didn't you?" We get to talking about a subject and I'm just right there with it; I'm all about it and the subject is so interesting. It makes me want to share what I know in class. It makes me want to take in more and discuss stuff.

I don't always want to be in that place. I don't want to take medicine forever. I want to get used to who I am.

Getting Organized

I keep saying that if I were only more organized, if I could have an infinite amount of space and an infinite amount of cool little things—a place for everything then everything would be fine and I could have a label on everything. I have dreams of a giant closet that has a place for every single thing so clothes don't end up on the floor—but they will.

My mother would never accept ADD as an excuse because she had the same problem. Anytime I would say, I can't handle this, I don't want to do this, ranting and raving on the floor at sixteen years old, she would say, "It's really hard but I did it. You just have to do it." I was, "I don't want to hear that anymore." But she had done it. She has developed this color-coding thing, making things look pretty is the way to do it. If it looks nice, it's easy, but it doesn't last very long.

There is a place for everything in my room. It's organized but I get so frustrated because things end up everywhere. It's always easier for me in the moment when I change my clothes to just throw them on the floor. I don't want to hang them up right now, that's not what I want to do right now. I'm taking my clothes off to go take a shower. I want to take a shower, I don't want to put my clothes away. That's just the way it is. When I first clean up, it's the mind-set of well, it's only one thing so it won't take me very long to clean up, and then a few days later, the room is such a mess anyway it doesn't matter if I throw it on the floor.

The one thing that worked for me my senior year was I stapled four sheets of paper together and I made a giant color-coded calendar, papers are blue, things that don't have to do with school are red, tests are orange. Just drawing on the thing so I see it every time I go into the room. The more complicated your life gets, you add envelopes with sticky notes and all that.

What I Need

I wanted an environment where I didn't feel stupid for wanting to learn and being interested in it and where in these small classes we spend a little bit of time every day doing hands-on stuff, whether it's taking trips to a certain place and learning about it that way—going to museums, going to the riverside to look at the geologic formations. Anything but reading out of a book that's from 1974 and doing stupid questions at the end.

Teachers and students have to see each other as whole people. I want teachers who know who I am. I think that's the most important thing, that they know me as a person and don't treat me like a number or a bother when I need extra help. It's important that I, Jessie, understand what we're talking about. I want teachers who are excited about the subject matter and they understand it and they have creative ways to present it.

It's so hard for me to do things that I don't want to do unless they're important and worthwhile and I'm going to get something out of them that's going to last longer than the grade. I don't even remember what I got last semester let alone years ago in high school. That wasn't enough for me.

I wouldn't choose to be born without ADD. I love who I am right now and I wouldn't want to change it."

Final Thoughts

My Sermon

How do I finish a book that has been part of my life and my soul for so long? How can I let it go, trusting that as you read it, you will hear what I'm trying to say? I'm asking you to treat all children as though they were yours; to love them, treasure them, and guide them with tenderness; to build relationships, listen, and be helpful.

It's not easy what you're being asked to do. You have pressures from all sides to meet mandates and raise test scores. In the midst of those pressures, mothers, fathers, grandparents, or guardians send to you the most precious thing they have, their children. They trust you to treat them with the utmost care and respect.

It is a moral imperative. Nothing is more important—not test scores, not grades, not a quiet, controlled classroom. Nothing is more important than having a child leave your classroom feeling lifted up and loved. Nothing is more important than challenging, guiding and encouraging the child to go farther than he or she ever thought possible.

With your help, students with ADHD can achieve their dreams rather than having them squashed and the children left broken. With your help, the singer sings, the writer writes, the scientist discovers, the dreamer continues to dream.

I've seen what happens to children when they are not lifted up. I've seen broken children; I've seen my son broken. I trusted the teachers I left him with; some of them betrayed that trust. I thank the ones who lifted him up. Denise, Dick, Brian, Amy, Mitch, Mrs. L., Mr. P., Donna B., Jeff B., Glo, Bob, and probably a few others saw something in Rob, cherished who he was, looked beyond the neurological anomaly to see that he was much more than that. Those were the teachers who listened to him and encouraged him to be the best that he could be.

For many ADHD students, school doesn't work. School is not very easy for these kids and it usually isn't very much fun. Students with ADHD are at high risk for dropping out and for drug and alcohol abuse. How can schools compete with the power and rush that those behaviors give kids?

I am convinced that we need more humor and joy, we need more listening, we need more relationship building, we need more innovative instruction, and we need more relevance in the curriculum. Are we teaching what kids really need to know? Is what we are teaching meaningful, exciting, and energizing? Will what we teach give students power over their thinking and their lives?

Can teachers challenge students and allow them to explore solutions to the questions they have about their lives and the world around them? Can we engage them in the process of inquiry? Can teachers create democratic classrooms where students have a choice and, more important, have a voice in their own learning?

It's difficult in the world of strict accountability, report cards, standardized tests, and state mandates. It's difficult in classrooms where organizational skills and conformity to one way of learning and thinking dominate. It's difficult in classes of twenty-five to thirty students where all are forced to march to the same drummer. It's difficult in a world where it is the amount of stuff you know that is important.

I wrote this book to help teachers understand their students who are challenged with ADHD. I wrote this book because the parents and guardians needed to have someone speak for them. I know the frustration of dealing with a child with ADHD. I've lived with it for years. I have done so with joy, laughter, frustration, sadness, anxiety, patience, humor, acceptance, and love. My son is more than lost cell phones, forgotten car payments, impounded cars, parking tickets by the dozens, a lost passport, a messy room, and lost keys. My son is an amazing, gentle, funny, smart, and talented young man.

We must open our hearts, our minds, and our ears to all the children in the classroom. We must listen to what they say to us and let them know that despite everything, the year they have with us will be one of the best they will ever have. We need to do the best we can to ensure that ADHD students acquire the skills and knowledge they need, while letting them know that they are valued, precious, and loved.

You have met the kids behind the label. Thank you for listening to the voices of those who live with ADHD every day of their lives. Thank you for entering their minds and hearts and truly hearing what they have to say. Thank you for never giving up.

Afterword

Storytellers Update

Throughout this book, you have had the opportunity to meet and listen to fourteen storytellers. Up to five years have passed since I interviewed them. Here's where they are now.

Kari

Kari was an eight-year-old third grader when I interviewed her. She had been diagnosed in the second grade and put on medication. She is now twelve and in the seventh grade. She loves performing in musicals at the community theater and playing her electric guitar. She also likes to play lacrosse, ski, and hang out with her friends. She still takes Adderall except on weekends or school vacations. Kari says, "ADHD affects the way I eat and feel. I've been on Adderall since second grade. When I don't take my meds, I'm wild and unfocused, talkative and loud. My friends tell me they like me better when I take my medication."

Nick

Nick was twenty years old when I interviewed him. He had dropped out of high school and hoped to get his GED. His dream was to play baseball. Nick is now twenty three. He received his GED and spent four semesters in college. He received a Freshman of the Year award in the baseball program. After the four semesters, Nick decided "college is not for me." He continues to play baseball at the county level. He is apprenticing as a builder and hopes to get licensed eventually. He plans to move to Florida where he hopes work will be plentiful and he will be able to play baseball more competitively and longer.

Geoff

Geoff, Nick's brother, was twenty-four years old when I first interviewed him. He had been working as a cabinetmaker for three years. He is now twenty seven. Geoff says, "I'm still working at the same place and am now Shop Floor Supervisor! I'm also getting married in October 2006! I'm still on Adderall." He went on to say: "After talking with you I realized how little I knew about ADD and bought a couple of books. Reading them (cover to cover) was incredibly good therapy for me. I still feel self-conscious about how bad of a speller I am. I know people are quick to judge intelligence based on it. Thank goodness for spellcheck."

Belkies

Belkies was a twenty-nine-year-old college senior when I interviewed her. She had been in college for about ten years, first at a community college and then at a four-year institution. Although she was not diagnosed with ADHD until college, she started having difficulties with school in kindergarten. After ten years, Belkies graduated from college. It was a thrilling moment to watch her walk across the stage.

Belkies works as a career counselor in a job training facility for adults age sixteen to twenty-four. At the facility, young people can receive vocational training, obtain a GED, work on a high school diploma, and/or obtain other job-related skills. In her job, Belkies tells her story to the people she works with. She serves as a model to them of what you can achieve if you keep at it. Belkies also works part time in an optician's office and she is training to be a licensed optician.

ADHD continues to affect her life. She says that sometimes she feels overwhelmed by work and will forget things. She deals with her ADHD by keeping herself busy. In addition to her two jobs, she coaches basketball. She still takes Ritalin but not on a regular basis. She is aware of when she needs it in order to concentrate and only takes it then. Belkies got married recently.

Kristina

Kristina was a seventeen-year-old high school junior when I interviewed her and her mother. She had received her diagnosis of ADHD during her sophomore year. Kristina says she had great hopes of receiving the help she would need to finish school after she was diagnosed. Unfortunately, she never did find the solution for overcoming her difficulties with getting things done and didn't finish high school. She would like to finish and is working with her high school to see what requirements she still needs to meet. She continues to have a difficult time getting the information that she knows into written form.

Kristina has worked at a couple of jobs since she left high school and has always been considered a model employee. Her dream is to do woodworking.

Kristina quit taking medication after her junior year in high school feeling that it changed her personality. She did accomplish one of her life goals. Kristina worked, saved money, bought a truck, and took a cross-country trip with her boyfriend.

Brandon

Brandon was one of the first people interviewed for this book. He was fourteen years old and in the ninth grade. Brandon was diagnosed and put on medication when he was in kindergarten.

Brandon is now nineteen years old. He graduated from high school with both a vocational degree and a traditional high school diploma. He tried college but realized it wasn't for him. He had been working for a company with a boss who understood his need for variety. Some impulsive decisions Brandon made on that job resulted in him being let go from the position, so he is currently unemployed.

Brandon personally made the choice to quit taking medication at age eighteen. His mother says he continues to be impulsive, forgetful, and a slob; constantly locks his keys in the car; and has had three auto accidents. But, she says, he is slowly maturing and beginning to take responsibility for his life.

Grant

When I interviewed Grant, he was a twenty-one-year-old college student studying film and directing. He was diagnosed with ADHD in the seventh grade.

Grant didn't complete his college degree. He left to try to make it in the world and figure out his life. He is now back in school at an arts conservatory working for a degree in film. He says he spends his time studying and working on movies.

He is still taking medication. Grant says that he has noticed that with age the effects of the medication are less noticeable. Through recognizing his needs, he has learned several ways to cope as well as different ways of studying and adapting. For example, when he has a test, he goes over his notes by himself once, makes flash cards, orders them and practices with them. Grant then gets together with two or three other people to study again. The key for him is to write everything down so that he can process it. Finally, he gets it straight by telling it to other people.

Grant has a couple more years in his program, but he feels that this time he's going to make it.

Jessie

Jessie was a twenty-one-year-old college senior when I interviewed her. She was diagnosed with ADHD her sophomore year in college.

She graduated from college in 2002 with a degree in Theatre and a minor in Honors Writing. She then moved to Tennessee where she enrolled in a two year Professional Actor Training Program. Jessie has had many jobs since she graduated including catering, which she liked because it involved variety, and being a teaching artist at a drama camp for kids.

Jessie still takes Adderall but not every day. The medication makes her very task-oriented, so she mostly takes it when she has to work and be very focused. She doesn't always like to be that way. Sometimes she enjoys letting herself wander and be drawn into doing the many things that her artistic side wants to do.

She says she is still trying to figure out what she's doing, and who and what she is. Jessie has many things she wants to do and is aware of the many options open to her. She knows that she wants to go to graduate school but doesn't know where or for what.

Jessie feels that she is increasingly taking responsibility for her life. She feels she is no longer a kid wanting to be an adult but an adult that sometimes still wants to act like a kid.

Nicholas

Nicholas was a twenty-two-year-old college senior studying engineering when he was interviewed. He had been diagnosed with ADHD in the third grade.

He graduated with his engineering degree and for the past year and a half has been working for a consulting engineering firm as an environmental engineer in the water division. Nicholas says, "I like what I do and I like who I work for and for that I am grateful. Having a supportive family along the way was probably most important in reaching my goals."

Nicholas went on to say, "I feel like ADD plays a big part in my everyday life as working full time requires a lot more time and focus than even engineering school did (for me, at least!). I have had to learn how to prioritize activities and focus on getting done what I need to do," he said, "while realizing that I may not be as productive timewise as most people. I suppose things have worked out fairly well for me nonetheless." Nicholas ended by saying, "I have no plans to seek medication or even advice on adult ADD. I just seem to 'go with the flow' and continue to do what I have been doing to this point."

Jillian

When I interviewed Jillian, she was an eighteen-year-old college freshman studying to be a teacher. She had been diagnosed with ADHD halfway through her sophomore year in high school.

She graduated from college with a major in History and Middle School/Secondary Education. Jillian wants to teach high school history and eventually be a college history professor. She did well in school (a 3.3 GPA), ran cross-country and track, was in both the History and Educational Honor Societies and was able to hold three jobs while doing her studies.

One of the major events in Jillian's life was a semester abroad in Ireland where she went to the University of Limerick. She also traveled throughout Europe during that semester.

Jillian says, "I have been able to come to grips with my ADHD. Looking back, three years ago, I shudder—a mere freshman. My maturity was still developing into adulthood." She still takes Concerta.

Jill

Jill was a nineteen-year-old college sophomore studying to be a teacher when I interviewed her. She had not had an official diagnosis.

Jill graduated with a B.S. degree in Education. She has been working as a teaching assistant in a second grade classroom. Jill dreams of being fully certified as a teacher but is having difficulty passing all the teacher tests required. She is continuing her studies in education in a post-bac program.

Dave

Dave had been an entertainer for more than twenty years when I interviewed him. He was self-diagnosed after having researched ADHD. After the interview, he went to see a doctor who felt, after a thorough screening, that Dave probably did not have ADHD but was suffering from depression.

Dave says, "What I had deemed as my ADD, from my research, are actually the symptoms that depression causes that happen to be shared with ADD. I have found the information in ADD materials very useful in attempting to understand myself and find solutions to challenges."

During the interview, I asked Dave how he would respond to people who asserted that ADHD wasn't real. He said, "I would say to them, 'That is fine. You can say that. Under the premise that it doesn't exist, you still have to address the symptoms. I believe that you have a neurotransmitter continuum of function and somewhere in there is depression and ADD and obsessive compulsive disorder.'" Dave feels that "It doesn't matter what you call it, there are still symptoms and people who need help so they can have a successful and happy life so they can function in society. You still have to figure something out."

Dave is still entertaining.

Jennie

Jennie was a twenty-one-year-old college senior studying to be a teacher when I interviewed her. She had been diagnosed with ADHD in high school.

Jennie graduated from college with a 3.985 GPA. She has worked as a substitute teacher and part-time reading tutor and is currently working as a special education paraprofessional in a second-grade class. Jennie is working toward her M.Ed, although hasn't decided whether it will be in Elementary Education, Special Education, or Reading.

Jennie married her college sweetheart in February of 2005, having dated for seven years. She says, "He has ADHD, as well, and it is always interesting! When my husband and I bought our current home, we bought a 'fixer-upper' and are struggling to fix it up. It's hard to get motivated sometimes—damn ADHD."

Jennie continued: "After college, I decided to no longer take Ritalin. I wanted to feel more in control over my own attention and self. Medication is not for everyone, and it sure helped me through some tough academic times, but I didn't want it anymore. I didn't want to feel like something was running/ruling my life." She said: "I felt like I was addicted. Even though I wasn't, I didn't like the feeling. Together with my doctor, I made an informed decision to go it alone. It's not easy some days, but I manage; yoga and meditation help!"

She says her husband still takes Adderall. "He says he couldn't function without it. He has a desk job, so it's more attention requiring than mine. I can tell you though that there are months bills get paid late or messages pile up and there doesn't seem to be an end in sight. It's the ADHD." She says it's hard, "but I fight each day, because

I want to be the fighter not have medicine fight for me. I know that's a strong statement, but one I came to on my own." She knows that "everyone's different. Sometimes we need someone to fight for us. Sometimes we need to be our own fighters. This is my time to fight for me. And, yes, everything is still color-coded."

Rob

My formal interviews with Rob happened when he was fourteen and eighteen. His entire life, however, is told throughout this book. Rob was diagnosed when he was in the sixth grade. He is now twenty-two years old.

Rob graduated from high school grateful that he would never have to do schooling again. Robert found a focus in the construction field and has spent the last three years preparing and pouring concrete foundations. He gets up and is off to work before anyone else in the house is awake and comes home after we've all eaten dinner. (He moved out and moved back home twice after seeing the reality of making it on his own.) He quit his job once and drove for a mail delivery service but commented, "When you're afraid to be alone with your thoughts, driving for a living is not a good job."

Rob's passion is his music. He has his own band that has been together since high school (with a few changes in musicians). Rob is the lead singer, plays rhythm guitar, and composes the majority of the songs. The band just recorded its third CD. They play at numerous venues throughout the Northeast. Rob hopes to someday make a living with his music. He says that's his destiny.

He still lives at home and even though I say I won't, I still pay some of his bills. The parking tickets eat up his paycheck.

References

American Psychiatric Association. 2000. *Diagnostic and Statistical Manual of Mental Disorders*, 4th Ed., Text Revision (DSM-IV-TR). Washington, DC: American Psychiatric Publishing, Inc.

Bizar, M., and H. Daniels. 2005. *Teaching the Best Practice Way: Methods That Matter, K–12*. Portland, ME: Stenhouse Publishers.

Daniels, H., A. Hyde, and S. Zemelman. 2005. *Best Practice: Today's Standards for Teaching and Learning in American Schools*, 3rd ed. Portsmouth, NH: Heinemann.

Davila, R., J. T. MacDonald, and M. L. Williams. 1991. "Memorandum to Chief State School Officers." Washington, DC: U.S. Department of Education, Office of Special Education and Rehabilitative Services.

Duff Dunlap, H., and R. Moss. 1995. *Why Johnny Can't Concentrate: Coping with Attention Deficit Problems*. New York: Bantam.

Gardner, H. 1983. *Frames of Mind*. New York: Basic Books.

McTighe, J., and G. Wiggins. 2005. *Understanding by Design*, expanded 2nd ed. Alexandria, VA: Association for Supervision and Curriculum Development.

Tomlinson, C. A. 2001. *How to Differentiate Instruction in Mixed-Ability Classrooms*, 2nd ed. Alexandria, VA: Association for Supervision and Curriculum Development.

Weiss, G., and L. Hechtman. 1993. *Hyperactive Children Grown Up: ADHD in Children, Adolescents, and Adults*, 2nd ed. New York: Guilford Press.

www.cdc.gov. 2003. "Mental Health in the United States: Prevalence of Diagnosis and Medication Treatment for Attention Deficit/ Hyperactivity Disorder."

www.chadd.org. 2000. "Evidence-Based Medication Management for Children and Adolescents with AD/HD." CHADD Fact Sheet #3.

Zeigler Dendy, C. A. 1995. *Teenagers with ADHD: A Parents' Guide*. Bethesda, MD: Woodbine House.

DATE DUE

JUL 0 7 2007	
AUG 2 2 2007	